CiViL WaR TaiLS

CiViL WaR TaiLS

8,000

cat soldiers tell the panoramic story

Ruth & Rebecca Brown

STACKPOLE
BOOKS
celebrating **90** *years*

Guilford, Connecticut

STACKPOLE BOOKS

Published by Stackpole Books
An imprint of The Rowman & Littlefield Publishing Group, Inc.
4501 Forbes Boulevard, Suite 200, Lanham, Maryland 20706
www.rowman.com

Distributed by
NATIONAL BOOK NETWORK
800-462-6420

British Library Cataloguing in Publication Information Available

Library of Congress Cataloging-in-Publication Data

ISBN 978-0-8117-1985-8 (paperback)
ISBN 978-0-8117-6591-6 (e-book)

♾™ The paper used in this publication meets the minimum
requirements of American National Standard for Information
Sciences—Permanence of Paper for Printed Library Materials,
ANSI/NISO Z39.48-1992

Printed in the United States of America

Contents

The Stories

WHY DO WE STUDY HISTORY? DOES IT HAVE ANY SIGNIFIcance for daily life? Do battle-fields really matter? Why do we preserve artifacts—bits and pieces from times and peoples long gone?

History is more than names and dates; it is the stories of living, breathing people of another time—people who had the same feelings, dreams, and fears that we have. As we read their stories, we can consider how they relate to us today.

This book is not a concise history of the Civil War. Instead, it tells stories—some well-known and some not. Come, take a journey through the dioramas of Civil War Tails at the Homestead Diorama Museum. See how individuals reacted when no one else would do the right thing, when destruction took everything they owned, or when death turned their world upside down. Ponder the similarities and connections between your life and the experiences of the men and women of the Civil War. How will their stories affect yours?

The Museum

IN JUNE 1995, REBECCA MADE TWO CLAY CATS AFTER READING *The Story of Robert E. Lee* by Iris Vinton and *The Story of Ulysses S. Grant* by Jeannette C. Nolan. One cat wore the gray uniform and beard of General Lee; the other wore the blue uniform and beard of General Grant.

At the time, we were eleven years old and we had always had cats as pets, so making the generals cats instead of people happened quite naturally. After making the generals, Rebecca made ten Rebels and ten Yankees. Those twenty-two cats sparked the fire of inspiration that resulted in more than 8,000 cats and nearly

The original cats

400 handmade horses, as of the writing of this book.

Rebecca admired how Generals Lee and "Stonewall" Jackson were strong Christians, so she chose to make the Confederates. Since we are twin sisters who do mostly everything together, Ruth made the Union soldiers. As we continued reading about

such as toothpicks for fence rails and cardboard for houses, rather than buying premade items. Regardless of its materials—cereal box or collectable die-cast model—a diorama can still inspire the viewer to think about the story portrayed.

Rebecca fell in love with Gettysburg early on and made a diorama of Pickett's Charge. For a couple of years, we worked to improve and enlarge it. In

the Civil War, whenever we came across an officer who piqued our interest, we made a cat to represent him. Finding a picture of the officer meant we could give the cat accurate facial hair.

At first, our growing armies fought as allies against our other toys, and then they fought each other, often ending up in big piles on our bedroom floor. Eventually, we tired of fixing saddles and bridles after every battle, so we began making stationary dioramas. Our first depicted First Bull Run, where Brig. Gen. Barnard Bee gave Thomas Jackson his nickname, "Stonewall." Accuracy in scale was not important to us at that point; we simply wanted to tell the story.

Another early diorama portrayed the 54th Massachusetts Regiment attacking Battery

Wagner in South Carolina. Progressing in our diorama building, we made the cats to scale. Still learning about materials, we built Battery Wagner out of our plastic Erector Set and covered it with clay.

Over the years, we have used whatever we had lying around,

2000, our diorama-making took a large step forward when we designed an entirely new, to-scale, topographical version. At over 40 square feet, "The Fate of Gettysburg" was our largest diorama. We made the cats as small as we could (1 inch tall) in order to squeeze as much of

Census Stats

Around 1999, Rebecca started keeping a census of the cats and horses in the two armies. Thanks to the census, we are able to identify "K-Cats," the cats marking every 1,000 cats. Sometimes, a K-Cat marks another milestone as well. We placed Cat 3000 on Battery Wagner at midnight on January 1, 2000. Five years later, we painted Cat 5000 on June 25—our tenth anniversary of making Civil War cats.

	US	CS	TOTAL
Cats	4,205	4,330	8,535
Horses	254	231	485

82% of our horses are handmade

Last Updated: 1/1/2018

the battleline as possible into the space available. Planning the layout, building the platform and topography, and making and setting up the soldiers and features took about four years.

In 2013, "The Fate of Gettysburg" became our second-largest diorama when we designed our 11-foot-long diorama of Little Round Top, "The Boys Are Still There." In the decade between these two dioramas, we had learned quite a bit about materials. So, instead of green paint for grass, we used "turf," which is a grass effect made from little specks of green or tan foam. Instead of store-bought trees, we used trees handmade by Ruth.

Instead of non-hardening modeling clay for the cats, we used Sculpey, a polymer clay designed to bake hard in a kitchen oven (or, as we found to our delight, a toaster oven for small batches). Again, we used cats that were as small as we could make—now ¾ inch tall.

While we keep track of "K-Cats," the numbers actually refer to how many cats we had at the moment of that cat's creation. Over the years, we have squashed in or given away many cats. Since it would be impossible to keep track of those who are no longer with us, we count only the ones we currently have.

The K-Cats

Number	Cat	Location	Photo
1000	Unknown	—	—
2000	Unknown	—	—
3000	Private (54th Massachusetts Infantry)	"I Want You to Prove Yourselves"	
4000	Private (CSA)	"The Fate of Gettysburg"	
5000	Brig. Gen. Will T. Martin	"Desperation at Skull Camp Bridge"	

The K-Cats

Number	Cat	Location	Photo
6000	Col. Joshua Chamberlain (20th Maine Infantry)	"The Boys Are Still There"	
7000	Acting Maj. Ellis Spear (20th Maine Infantry)	"The Boys Are Still There"	
8000	Artilleryman (Battery A)	"The Fate of Gettysburg"	

museum, and within a year had moved to Gettysburg. In 2015, Civil War Tails opened, starting our cats on a new adventure that was only a child's dream twenty years before.

WHY CATS?

When we began making our soldiers, it was just for fun, and making them cats came naturally. Growing up, we often pretended to be cats, even when playing Robin Hood, which is probably where our "cat-ification" of people began. Not until we began displaying our dioramas did we have to answer the question "Why cats?" Now that we have a museum, this question takes on a new aspect: why cats and why still cats? Aside from the fact that replacing them with people would be an enormous (and expensive) task, we believe our cats have much to offer, as cats.

As we planned our museum, we discussed how much to emphasize the cat aspect. It may sound strange, but we do not want our cats to be "cutesy" and trivialize the soldiers. Instead, every cat is in a human pose (none stand on all four paws). The wounded have human wounds (no bloody tails). Details such as insignia on Confederate officers are as accurate as on a human figure.

Every diorama is a new venture on the learning curve. But old dioramas still tell their stories and serve as examples for children to learn that dioramas do not have to be detailed, complicated, or intimidating to make.

How did our dioramas move from a childhood hobby to a museum? In high school, we taught Civil War lessons to homeschoolers, using our cats as visual aids, and we displayed our dioramas annually at the retirement community where we worked. Every year, one resident suggested, "You should take them into schools!" Thanks to the positive reactions from both students and residents, in 2012, we began to seriously consider a

Just as artists use the mediums of photography or recycled metal to portray their messages, we use our cats as a medium to tell stories of the Civil War.

But even if we have *our* mindset right, do our visitors see soldiers or cats? One thing we enjoy about running a museum is observing the different ways people view our dioramas. Licensed battlefield guides enjoy seeing historical details and appreciate a chance to *see* the fighting that they can only read about now, 150 years after the fact. One visitor was thrilled to see USS *Monitor* populated by the officers and men he had studied so thoroughly.

We use cats as our medium to tell inspiring stories of the Civil War.

On the other end of the spectrum, some people come to see the cats and end up being affected in a way that they did not expect. One visitor commented that seeing the dead and wounded would not have affected her if the figures were humans, but something about

seeing bleeding kitties had an impact on her and gave her an appreciation for what the *men* went through. Another left the museum inspired to read more stories of the men and women of the Civil War.

And some people never even notice the tails!

How people learn is another aspect where our cats can help. Some of us prefer books, some prefer hands-on learning. So, while we might enjoy every page of Harry Pfanz's excellent books on Gettysburg, other people might never get past page one. Yet our dioramas fascinate them. Perhaps they like the tiny figures, perhaps the detail catches

Capt. Michael Spessard

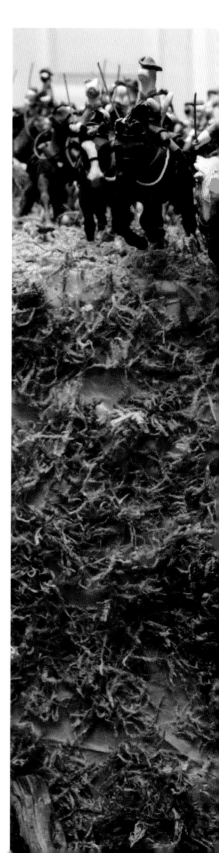

their attention, or perhaps the idea of a moment frozen in time intrigues them. Whatever the initial reason, once the dioramas draw them in, those visitors find themselves interested by the stories of the men.

So, why cats? Just as they excited students and retirees alike in the early 2000s, our cats' mission today remains unchanged: to share stories of the Civil War and draw in people who otherwise would never think twice about our nation's history.

UNDERSTANDING WAR THROUGH DIORAMAS?

Someone once asked us how dioramas can help us understand war in general. We believe the answer depends on the focus of the diorama. Many focus on the *overall* battle or story. In contrast, our dioramas tell stories of *individuals*. Through these portrayals, we can relate to these people, even 150 years later.

Take for example Capt. Michael Spessard, who had just seen his son fall mortally wounded during Pickett's Charge. Is any parent surprised

that when this irate father reaches the Union lines, he chases away three would-be captors, pelting them with rocks? Or consider Sgt. Andrew Tozier—growing up with an abusive, alcoholic father but going on to earn the Medal of Honor at Gettysburg. How many kids nowadays need to hear his story and learn that their character—not the past—dictates their future and potential?

Studying war, you find yourself in a strange clash between destruction and glory, pain and valor, death and salvation. Amid all the stories of blood, you also find stories of rescue and relief. And that is why we keep studying war. It is not for the stories of destruction, but for the stories of hope and determination, of men standing firm, doing what is right and helping others, of man at his best.

If you let those stories sink in, you can't help but think "Would I do that? *Could* I do that?" If our dioramas can interest people in *those* stories and inspire them to be the type of person who puts others before themselves when trouble comes, our cats will have done their work.

The Bombardment of Fort Sumter

IN LATE 1860, THE PEOPLE OF CHARLESTON, SOUTH CAROLINA, WERE ENTHUS-iastic about the idea of secession. This put Maj. Robert Anderson in a bind. As an officer of the United States Army commanding the small garrison in Charleston Harbor, he had a duty to protect federal property there. But the government in Washington, D.C., had told him he must avoid riling the South Carolinians to the point of war. The fate of the nation rested on his shoulders. How could Major Anderson do his duty as a soldier and still maintain the status quo?

Anderson and his men were stationed in Fort Moultrie, which had been so buried in drifting sand that cattle occasionally wandered in over the walls, and which was now torn apart for renovations. Homes sprawling from Moultrieville would provide excellent nests for snipers to fire into the fort. Yet the other forts around the harbor were no more defensible. Castle Pinckney, on Shute's Folly Island about three-quarters of a mile east of the city's docks, was manned by one ordnance sergeant, his wife, and his fifteen-year-old daughter. Across the harbor from Fort Moultrie sat the ruins of Fort Johnson, a relic from the Revolutionary War.

That left Fort Sumter.

Sitting in the middle of the harbor on a man-made island of over a hundred thousand tons of stone, Fort Sumter could have been the strongest fort along the South Atlantic coast. If occupied by federal soldiers, the fort could close the harbor and strangle

The fate of the nation rested on Major Anderson's shoulders.

Charleston's trade. If taken by South Carolinians, Fort Sumter could pound Anderson's small force in Fort Moultrie and close the harbor to naval support.

"The Bombardment of Fort Sumter"

Scale: 1:96

Number of Cats:
US: 100

Dimensions:
5'2" x 4'4.5"

Date Created:
2011–2012

This was Fort Sumter's potential—not the reality. Even after thirty years of building efforts and a recent flurry of activity that had Charleston watching with suspicion, Fort Sumter remained unfinished.

It did not have the intended 146 guns mounted, and Anderson had nowhere near 650 men to garrison the fort. Still, Anderson made efforts to finish Fort Sumter as well as repair Fort Moultrie and Castle Pinckney. But whenever he tried to strengthen his position, fears of war thwarted his efforts. He begged the administration

Gun barrels awaiting placement

Maj. Robert Anderson

in Washington for reinforcements, but they did not come, since granting his request might be considered Northern "aggression" and touch off civil war. He tried taking supplies from the U.S. Army arsenal in Charleston, but that so infuriated the Charlestonians that the administration ordered him to return the firearms.

On December 11, 1860, Anderson received authorization from Secretary of War John Floyd to move his men into the most appropriate fort if he had "tangible evidence of a design to proceed to a hostile act." But what did that mean? With tensions high and too few men to man the three primary fortresses in Charleston Harbor, Anderson longed to move into Fort Sumter. But would that be

Anderson had to take the fort before the Charlestonians.

considered a hostile military move and tip the nation over the brink into war? If it did, Anderson would be the one blamed. Or should he stay in Fort Moultrie, risking defeat and criticism—or worse—for not escaping the trap?

Then, on December 20, South Carolina seceded. More boats than usual patrolled the harbor and snooped around Fort Sumter at night. Anderson had to take the fort before the Charlestonians did. At dusk on December 26, the federal garrison slipped into Fort Sumter in a move so secret that even Anderson's officers did not know about the plan until that day.

In the following months, the Confederates occupied the empty forts surrounding the harbor and built other fortified positions, including a "floating battery" of heavy guns.

Making Fort Sumter Defensible

When the federal garrison moved into Fort Sumter, they began urgent efforts to make the fort defensible. The fort had three levels, called "tiers." Guns had not been mounted on the second (middle) tier, so the men filled the unfinished embrasures with masonry and lumber.

The men mounted cannons on the barbette (top) tier and on the first (bottom) tier. They mounted two 10-inch and four 8-inch Columbiads as mortars in the parade ground.

Fort Sumter's weakest part was its gate; to protect against the Confederates landing boats at the wharf and esplanade at the rear of the fort, the defenders laid mines around the wharf and mounted two 8-inch howitzers at the gate.

They reinforced the gate itself with 3-foot-thick masonry, leaving a man-sized hole, and set up "fougasses," stone piles charged with gunpowder that could be detonated from inside the fort.

On the barbette tier, the defenders notched out part of the wall so a cannon could cover the wharf.

Above the gate, they built wooden platform boxes, called "machicoulis galleries," with holes in the floor so they could shoot into attackers and even drop grenades (shells modified for use with a lanyard).

Inside, the defenders removed the stone flagging from the parade so that enemy shells would plow into the dirt and cause less damage when they exploded.

Traverses made of piles of dirt and other materials shielded the gate and various areas of the fort from enemy fire.

Most of these defensive features appear in photographs that the Confederates took after the surrender. We found those photographs indispensable as we made our diorama recreating the second day of the bombardment. ★

Moving to Fort Sumter did not lessen the psychological burden on Anderson. By the time the fort surrendered, in April 1861, the months in Charleston Harbor had taken such a toll on Anderson's health that he could not participate for long in the war that came. After struggling with the fate of the nation upon his shoulders, Major Anderson never fully recovered.

At about 4:30 A.M. on April 12, 1861, an artillery shot boomed over Charleston Harbor from a mortar battery at Fort Johnson. Then a Columbiad thundered from the Iron Battery on Cummings Point. Then all of the Confederate batteries opened fire, jarring the residents of Charleston awake. Some hurried to watch the display from their rooftops.

One resident recalled praying "as I never prayed before."

These first shots of the Civil War were aimed at the dark hulk of Fort Sumter. The day before, Brig. Gen. Pierre G. T. Beauregard had demanded the fort's evacuation, but Major Anderson refused. Just before 1:00 A.M. on April 12, Beauregard sent another boat to the fort to ask how long before

the garrison would be starved out. After discussion with his officers, Anderson told the emissaries that he would evacuate at noon on April 15 if he had not received controlling instructions from the government or additional supplies. Dissatisfied with this response, the Confederates said they would open fire in one hour.

Fort Sumter did not immediately respond to the bombardment. When morning came, the men formed, called roll, and had breakfast: fat pork and water. Since December, the situation in the fort had steadily deteriorated. While the government expected Major Anderson to hold Fort Sumter, they would not send the supplies and reinforcements he so desperately needed. So, as provisions dwindled, the men scrounged up what they could. On April 11, the last bread was eaten, leaving only salt pork and a few crackers. The men sifted broken glass out of moldy rice that had been drying since February. One man tucked away a potato that Surgeon Samuel Crawford recalled had been "tramped on," but "not hurt . . . much."

Without reinforcements, Anderson had no lives to spare. Of the 128 men in the fort, 43 were civilian workmen and 8 were musicians. Only 68 were enlisted men, with 9 officers over them. Anderson had instructed his officers to use only the sheltered guns in the first tier; guns mounted on the barbette tier were too exposed to enemy fire. This limited the effectiveness of the fire returned from the fort. The 32-pounders and three 42-pounders in the lower tier were not powerful enough to inflict serious damage on Confederate positions.

In contrast, the Columbiads on the barbette tier were mounted at better angles and could fire projectiles weighing 128 pounds.

Anderson divided his men into three details under Capt. Abner Doubleday, Lt. Jefferson C. Davis (not the Confederate president), and Surgeon Crawford, who also knew artillery. A little before 7:00 A.M., Doubleday's detail fired Fort Sumter's first shot at Cummings Point to the south. Davis's detail fired westward at mortars on James Island.

Confederates warned they would open fire in one hour.

What Happened To Those Guns?

On one side of our diorama, a Columbiad and a howitzer lie dismounted, the Columbiad's barrel halfway into the stair tower. We recreated the positions using Confederate photographs. What happened to those guns? We believe we pieced together the answer as we built the diorama.

The ineffectiveness of the smaller cannons on the first tier frustrated Fort Sumter's garrison. One story tells how two sergeants snuck upstairs against orders and fired the 10-inch Columbiad on the right face at the Iron Battery. After reloading, the two men could not throw the gun carriage in gear to run the gun forward because that required six men. So, they fired the gun "from battery," meaning from the recoiled position. The second recoil flipped the 8-ton monster over backwards, sending the gun barrel halfway into the stair tower and dismounting the 8-inch howitzer nearby. The resulting jumbled mess is visible in the foreground of a Confederate photograph. ★

Crawford's detail faced northeast to the floating battery anchored at Sullivan's Island, but later moved to three guns bearing on Fort Moultrie, which lay farther down the island.

As the bombardment continued, Confederate shot smashed the officers' quarters along the back of the fort and the barracks on either side. Made of brick, these buildings were supposedly fireproof. But the Confederates used heated cannonballs called "hot shot," and the wooden structure inside the buildings ignited. Workmen put out that fire, but another soon raged out of control.

By noon, Anderson limited firing to six guns as the fort ran low on the cartridge bags that held gunpowder for each shot. Workmen and musicians busily sewed cartridge bags out of shirts and blankets with the fort's six needles.

In the early afternoon, the Union soldiers spotted the long-awaited Union fleet outside the harbor—but the ships did not come to help. When the garrison dipped the colors as a signal to the ships, a shot cut the halyards, and the flag jammed at half-staff.

One shot sliced the halyard and jammed the flag at half-staff.

Meanwhile, shots punctured the cisterns above the barracks, sending water over the flames. At 7:00 P.M. a rainstorm put out the remaining fires.

As darkness descended, the fort's guns fell silent to conserve cartridge bags. All night, the garrison waited for the fleet to come help them, but to their disgust, the ships just sat there. The men could not know that the fleet waited for a larger, stronger ship that had actually been redirected to Florida.

The rain ended by about 8:00 A.M., and April 13 cleared to a warm day with vivid blue water. But thunder still rolled over the harbor, and the inside of Fort Sumter remained a fiery hell of billowing smoke and shrieking, exploding shells.

As the morning wore on, the traverse protecting the main gate crumbled, and the gate took direct hits from the Iron

Battery on Cummings Point. The barracks caught fire again. Major Anderson finally ordered the men to let the buildings burn, but the fire crept closer and closer to the powder magazine in the ground floor of the officers' quarters. To make the situation worse, powder had leaked in a trail that led, like a fuse, to the 275 barrels of gunpowder stored there. Fire in the magazine could explode the fort.

Every man except those on the gun crews rushed to save the gunpowder. Hacking at the burning woodwork with axes did not stop the fire, so the men formed a line and rolled barrels across the

Every soldier rushed to save the gunpowder before it could explode the entire fort.

parade ground—amid falling shells bursting in the dirt—to casemates on the other side.

They saved 50 to 100 barrels before burning debris began to fall around them and they had to close the copper door and

hope for the best. They dug a trench in front of the magazine and banked the door with dirt.

The fort ran so low on cartridges that Anderson ordered only one gun fired every ten minutes.

Grenades and shells piled along the rear gorge wall began to explode as the barracks fire spread. Fiery particles drifting into the casemates threatened the salvaged gunpowder. The men covered five barrels with wet blankets and dumped the rest out of the fort through gun embrasures. Then a shot jammed the magazine door, so the only available powder was in those five barrels.

Capt. Abner Doubleday times a shot.

They ran so low on cartridges that Anderson ordered only one gun fired every ten minutes.

Surgeon Crawford climbed to the barbette tier to check on the fleet—only to find that it still waited outside the bar. Meanwhile, the situation inside the fort worsened. The men used socks as cartridge bags because there was nothing else left to hold powder. Burning debris fell all around. The gate was on fire.

Solid shot pummeled the brick stair towers until they crumbled. Shells exploded inside the fort, showering every exposed surface with chunks of brick and shards of glass along with shell fragments. The jettisoned powder barrels exploded outside the fort. Smoke billowed into the casemates where the

men worked the guns, forcing some men to sit outside the fort so they could breathe.

Shortly before 1:00 P.M., a shot smashed the flagstaff. Lt. Norman J. Hall raced through the flames to save the fallen flag. Fire singed his hair and eyebrows, and his gilt epaulettes became so hot he had to tear them off, but he emerged with the flag, beating out its smoldering edges. Major Anderson's old friend Peter Hart found a long spar and, with the help of a few men, raised the flag again on the parapet.

Seeing the flag go down, Confederate colonel Louis Wigfall hurried over to the fort to negotiate surrender, even though he had no authority to do so. Anderson discussed surrender and finally agreed under previously offered terms. After Wigfall left, other officers came—this time from General Beauregard.

Learning that Wigfall had had no authority to accept his surrender, Major Anderson announced that the fort would not surrender after all. The authorized officers convinced him to talk to them and ultimately extended the same terms anyway. They agreed that Anderson and his men would leave the next day. Amazingly, the battle ended with only four men wounded on each side, and one horse killed.

Loyal to the end to his flag and his nation, Major Anderson intended to leave the fort with a 100-gun salute. However, a gun discharged early during the salute, killing Pvt. Daniel Hough and wounding five other men when the shot set off nearby cartridges. As a result, the salute was shortened to fifty guns. Private Hough was buried with honors in the parade. Pvt. Edward Galloway died of his wounds five days later.

At 4:00 P.M. on April 14, 1861, Major Anderson's men marched out of the fort to the tune of "Yankee Doodle" and boarded the steamer *Isabel*. Anderson bore the garrison flag under his arm. He would raise the flag over the fort again four years later, on April 14, 1865, upon the end of the Civil War. President Abraham Lincoln was invited to that ceremony, but he declined, choosing instead to accompany his wife to Ford's Theater.

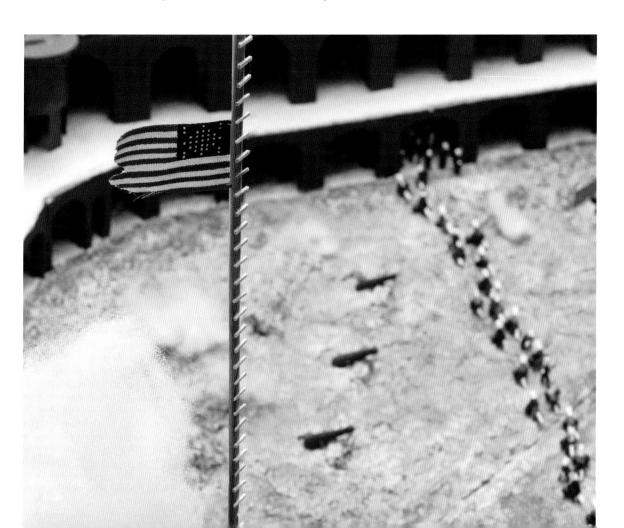

The Ironclads

BOTH THE NORTH AND THE SOUTH GAVE THOUGHT TO IRON-clad ships early in the war, but the young Confederacy had more incentive to move forward with the idea. Northern ships blockaded southern ports, keeping supplies from coming in and commerce from going out. The Confederacy needed to break this stranglehold, but it did not have the resources to make or acquire ships to defeat the U.S. Navy. The Confederates needed to think creatively. Would not a few impregnable ships be as good as—or better than—a fleet of wooden ships?

In building their first ironclad, the Confederates used the hull of USS *Merrimack*, which had been burned and scuttled on the night of April 21, 1861, when the Norfolk Navy Yard in Virginia was evacuated. *Merrimack* sank so quickly that the fire went out before her engines and hull were damaged, so the Confederates raised her, cut off the burned top portions of her hull, and built an entirely different ship. Rechristened CSS *Virginia*, the ship was nevertheless often referred to as *Merrimack*, after the original.

Once the South began work on an ironclad, the North hurried to design and build an ironclad of its own. One of the approved designs came from Swedish engineer John Ericsson and would be named *Monitor*. This design combined elements from other vessels into a unique craft that also incorporated new technology,

Wouldn't a few iron ships be better than a whole fleet of wooden ships?

such as a revolving turret, screw propeller, and steam power. Other innovations included a forced-draft air system to

"The Horrid Creation of a Nightmare v. the Little Pygmy"

Scale: 1:96

Number of Cats:
US: 21; CS: 190

Dimensions:
4'3" x 2'3"

Date Created:
July 7, 2012–Aug. 15, 2014

feed fresh air to the boilers and living spaces, and a new system for eliminating ship's waste underwater that would later be used in submarines.

Virginia and *Monitor* were unique and weird compared to the traditional ships of their day, but they also could not have been more different from each other.

Crewed by 320 men and about 262 feet long, *Virginia* had a draft of about 22 feet when fully loaded.

Underwater, she would have looked like a normal ship, except for the 2-foot-long ram on her bow and the flat deck or "fantail" over her stern. Shaped like a platypus bill, the fantail protected *Virginia*'s propeller and rudder.

Above water, *Virginia* looked nothing like an ordinary ship. She had no masts and hardly anything visible at her bow and stern. In her middle rose a great, armored casemate with sides set at a 36-degree slope to deflect incoming shot. Shaped like the roof of a house, the casemate extended about 6 inches below the surface of the water in "eaves" and consisted of a 2-foot-thick backing of oak and pine, covered with two layers of 1- and 2-inch iron plate. A conical pilothouse sat on top of the casemate's forward end, and a single smokestack rose in the middle.

Inside *Virginia*'s casemate sat six 9-inch Dahlgren guns, two 7-inch Brooke rifles set as

USS *Monitor*

AUTHOR'S COLLECTION

pivot guns, and two 6.4-inch Brooke rifles. Two of the Dahlgrens had been fitted for firing hot shot, but otherwise *Virginia* carried explosive shells instead of solid shot due to delays and the expectation that she would face only wooden ships.

Carrying fifty-eight officers and men, *Monitor* was about two-thirds of *Virginia*'s length with a draft of only 11 feet, 4 inches. Even the slightest waves washed over *Monitor*'s raftlike upper deck, which rode a little over a foot above the waterline. Iron plate covered the 172-foot-long deck and the sides of the 124-foot-long lower hull.

An overhanging "skirt" of iron surrounded the raft to protect the hull, propeller, and rudder from ramming by another ship.

With this extremely low profile, only the turret and little pilothouse would be visible to a casual observer, making *Monitor* look like a pillbox or cheesebox on a floating shingle. *Monitor*'s turret was made of eight layers of 1-inch-thick curved iron plate with an extra inch around

The turret and pilothouse

the gun ports. Twenty feet in diameter and nine feet tall, the turret weighed 120 tons *without* the guns inside. On the forward part of the deck, the tiny pilothouse stood 4 feet high with an eye slit ⅝ inch tall. The pilothouse was not high enough for good visibility but *was* tall enough to be hit if the ship's own guns fired straight ahead.

THE CONTRAST BETWEEN THE IRON-clads led observers to conclude that *Monitor*—"that little thing"—was "no match for the great monster!" *Virginia*

was a "huge, half submerged crocodile," a giant, or the leviathan. In contrast, *Monitor* was "the reverse of formidable," "small and trifling," "insignificant . . . a speck on the dark blue sea at night, almost a laughable object by day."

One survivor of the frigate USS *Congress* admitted that before the two ironclads met in battle, "we did not have much faith in the 'Monitor.'" When *Virginia*'s Midshipman Hardin B. Littlepage first saw the Union ironclad, he thought he saw a raft carrying a frigate's boiler. Observing *Monitor*'s first shot, Littlepage thought the boiler had exploded . . . until the projectile hit *Virginia*.

THE BATTLE

On March 8, 1862, a bright sun shone out of a clear sky onto the blockading U.S. Navy flotilla sitting at anchor in Hampton Roads, Virginia. The flotilla included the 50-gun frigate USS *Congress*, the 24-gun sloop of war USS *Cumberland*, and, some miles away, the 47-gun frigate USS *Minnesota* and the 46-gun frigate USS *Roanoke*, which was the squadron flagship but awaited repairs to a broken propeller shaft. These ships could meet anything the Confederates wanted to throw at them, but all was quiet this day. A gentle breeze wafted over the water to flutter the Saturday laundry drying on the ships' rigging, and men went about their business.

At about 12:40 P.M., sailors on *Cumberland* and *Congress* noticed a column of black smoke in the distance. As it became apparent

that the Confederates were coming, drums beat to quarters and men sprang into action. Sailors scurried to pull down their laundry and set topsails. Gun crews loaded and ran out their guns. Freshly scattered sand crunched under their feet, ready to provide footing and soak up the blood that would pool on the decks. Tugboats steamed over to tow the ships into position.

At 1:08 P.M., upon seeing a lookout vessel's signal flag alerting them to the enemy's approach, *Minnesota* fired up her boilers and *Roanoke* signaled for a tugboat's help. A couple of minutes later, the Confederate ironclad CSS *Virginia* appeared.

At first glance, *Virginia*'s mission looked like madness. Capt.

The great black ironclad approached the Union ships in silence.

Franklin Buchanan intended to take on a naval squadron totaling 188 guns with a mere 27 guns between his *Virginia* and her band of little gunboats. He planned to deal with *Cumberland* and *Congress* first, and then *Minnesota* and *Roanoke*.

As it turned out, *Virginia* had quite enough guns for the job.

The great black ironclad approached the Union ships in

silence as smaller craft scurried, in the words of *Virginia*'s chief engineer, "like chickens on the approach of a hovering hawk." She made no reply as *Congress*, *Cumberland*, and shore batteries opened fire. Their shots glanced off her casemate with no apparent effect. Now, the Union men knew they were in for a fight, the likes of which they had never seen before. Even a point-blank broadside did nothing to the ironclad. Still, she kept coming. Still, she made no reply.

At last, within a mile of *Cumberland*, *Virginia*'s bow pivot gun spoke. The exploding shell wounded several marines on *Cumberland*. The wooden ship hurled back a broadside in response. It had no effect upon *Virginia*.

Again, *Virginia*'s bow pivot gun spoke. This second shot killed an entire gun crew on *Cumberland*, except for the powder boy and the gun captain, whose arms were ripped off. Those two shots from the ironclad grimly presaged the outcome of the day's battle.

By 2:30 P.M., *Virginia* was 300 yards away from *Cumberland*, which remained at anchor. As *Virginia* passed *Congress*, the ironclad's starboard guns opened fire. A single shot dismounted one of *Congress*'s guns and killed or wounded the gun crew. Other shots started fires that threatened the powder magazine and, in the words of *Congress*'s surgeon, changed the frigate's "handsome gun deck . . . into a slaughter pen."

Virginia continued inexorably toward *Cumberland*, in the words of a news correspondent, "weird and mysterious, like some devilish and superhuman monster, or the horrid creation of a nightmare."

Even as the wooden ship's shots bounced off the ironclad with "no more effect than peas from a pop-gun," *Virginia*'s replies shattered wood and slaughtered men. In *Cumberland*'s forward division alone, every first and second gun captain was either killed or wounded.

Driving forward with her great mass, *Virginia* plowed her ram into *Cumberland*'s side, opening a hole 7 feet wide. The sloop began to sink by the starboard bow, but for the next half-hour, *Cumberland*'s crew continued to work their guns and raised ammunition before inrushing water could wet the powder.

Shots from *Cumberland* tore the ends off the barrels of two of *Virginia*'s guns, swept away anchors and boats, riddled the smokestack, and killed or wounded several men.

The crews continued to work the damaged guns on *Virginia*, but they had to beat out flames in the casemate's wooden backing after each shot. The heat from *Cumberland*'s shots set fire to the pork fat spread over *Virginia*'s casemate to make projectiles glance off her more easily. Midshipman Littlepage on *Virginia* recalled, "It seemed she was literally frying from one end to the other."

Gunpowder clung to the sweaty faces of the gun crews and turned their shirtless bodies black. Guns roared and slammed backward. Smoke rolled into the casemate, filling noses and mouths with its sulfurous stench. Enemy shots crashed into the iron and bounded away. Men who leaned against the casemate fell sprawling, bleeding at the ears, from the concussion of projectiles hitting the outside iron. Still, the men enthusiastically worked their guns and shouted to each other comments like "Jack, don't this smell like hell?"

Meanwhile, *Cumberland*'s wounded below deck drowned as the Union ship filled with

Enemy shots crashed into the iron and bounded away.

water. Splinters, blood, and mangled corpses covered the decks. Death and destruction whittled down gun crews until it became difficult to muster enough men to work the guns. At *Cumberland*'s forward pivot gun, Acting Master William Kennison and his crew furiously loaded and fired, sloshing about in water that crept up to their knees, then gradually over the muzzle of their gun.

At 3:35 P.M., *Cumberland* lurched over to port. Finally, the order came to abandon ship. Of 376 men aboard *Cumberland*, 121 were killed and 30 wounded. Lt. John Taylor Wood aboard *Virginia* concluded of his valiant opponent "No ship was ever fought more gallantly."

Virginia now faced *Congress*, which was promptly towed into water too shallow for *Virginia*. The Confederate ironclad positioned herself off *Congress*'s stern and pummeled the frigate. Shells

tore through the length of the ship, dismounting guns, starting fires, mangling sailors, and killing her commanding officer.

Beached at the wrong angle and with her stern guns disabled, *Congress* struggled to bring any guns to bear on the ironclad. After about an hour, with blood running from her scuppers onto a nearby tugboat, *Congress* surrendered to avoid further loss of life. At the end of the day, of the 434 men on *Congress*, 110 were killed and 26 wounded, of whom 10 would later die.

As the Confederates accepted *Congress*'s surrender and

The gun crews had stopped firing "out of pity" for the shattered ship.

transferred wounded from the burning ship, infantry and artillery on shore opened fire on the Confederates, reasoning that although the Navy had surrendered, they had not. Furious at this breach of civilized warfare, Captain Buchanan ordered

Congress burned. He was so enraged that he climbed onto *Virginia*'s top deck and started shooting at the shore with a carbine. Enemy fire wounded him in the thigh, and Lt. Catesby Jones, *Virginia*'s executive officer, took command. The ironclad peppered *Congress* with hot shot until about 5:00 P.M., when, as Lt. J. R. Eggleston recalled, the gun crews stopped firing, without orders, "out of pity" for the shattered wooden ship.

With *Congress* aflame, *Virginia* and two of her gunboats fired on the grounded *Minnesota* until about 6:30 P.M., when darkness and the receding tide forced the Confederates to withdraw for the night.

While Union casualties totaled some 325 killed and wounded between ships and shore, Confederate casualties totaled 27. Of those, the ironclad herself suffered only 2 killed and 8 wounded.

As *Congress* continued to burn, a pilot on *Virginia* saw a low, strange-looking vessel glide through the firelight. A Northern reporter in Fort Monroe remembered, "All at once a speck of light gleamed on the distant wave. It moved; it came nearer and nearer." And then—"*the Monitor appeared*."

Earlier, about 4:00 P.M., while *Congress* fought for her life, *Monitor*'s crew heard the distant booming of heavy guns as they passed Cape Henry.

About fifteen miles from their destination, they nevertheless stripped their ship of her sea-rig, keyed up the turret, and prepared for battle.

As *Monitor* approached Hampton Roads, her crew learned of the destruction to the squadron. Then it seemed to the men that *Monitor* crept along as they helplessly stared ahead at the puffs of smoke that marked exploding shells and later, as night fell, the distant flashes of cannon fire. They passed sail and steamships fleeing Hampton Roads. Finally, they saw *Congress* engulfed in flames.

Monitor arrived at about 9:00 P.M. and anchored off *Roanoke*. The ironclad's commanding officer, Lt. John Lorimer Worden, reported to Comm. John Marston on *Roanoke* and

agreed to stay despite orders to go to Washington, D.C.

BY 1:00 A.M., *MONITOR* HAD TAKEN UP A POSITION ALONGSIDE *Minnesota* with the mission of protecting the grounded frigate. Soon after, the little ironclad's crew experienced a sobering reminder of the destruction that awaited them the next day, as *Congress* exploded, shaking buildings for miles around and showering fragments as far as 7 miles.

Monitor did not inspire much hope or confidence. *Minnesota* towered over her, and the idea that two guns could prevail where scores of guns had had no effect must have seemed preposterous. *Monitor* was no savior; she was an appetizer.

Providence

As with any battle, many seemingly random occurrences converged to bring about the battle between the ironclads. Captain Buchanan postponed his attack for one day because of a storm. If not for that delay, *Virginia* would have had two full days to destroy the Union flotilla and then return safely to Norfolk before *Monitor* even arrived.

Meanwhile, *Monitor* left New York for Virginia on March 6, following orders from February 20. Just hours after her departure, an order came for her to proceed to Washington, D.C. But Lieutenant Worden did not receive that order until *Monitor* arrived in Hampton Roads. If he had received it earlier, he would have gone to Washington without question, dooming the flotilla. Instead, he discussed the matter with Commodore Marston, who recognized that the order was out of date. Despite the training ingrained in him after forty-eight years in the service, Marston had the courage and common sense to propose that *Monitor* stay and protect *Minnesota*.

Ironically, *Virginia* almost did not survive long enough to face *Monitor*. When *Virginia* rammed *Cumberland*, her ram became stuck as the wooden ship sank. *Cumberland* began to pull the ironclad down with her. Chief Engineer H. Ashton Ramsay pushed *Virginia*'s engines to the limit, but the engines' power did not save *Virginia*. The tide turned the ironclad nearly parallel to her victim, and the ram, improperly secured to the hull due to a damaged casting, twisted off. At the same time, a swell rolled *Cumberland* and relieved the pressure on the ram, enabling *Virginia* to back away.

History is a convergence of events. Some may seem unimportant when they happen, but later, their effects can make all the difference. Factors such as timing and nature affected whether *Monitor* showed up in Hampton Roads at all and whether *Virginia* survived to face her or simply became an ironclad sunk by a wooden ship. While reading history, keep an eye open for little details that weave together and influence the outcome of major events. ★

Dawn on March 9 promised another beautiful day to anyone but the Union forces in Hampton Roads. The grounded Union ships waited helplessly for *Virginia*'s approach. While *Virginia*'s crew enjoyed a celebratory breakfast that even included a bit of whiskey, the crew on *Monitor*—most of them having been up for forty-eight hours trying to keep their ship afloat in storms down the coast—munched cold biscuits in a daze and endured wisecracks and derision from everyone around them. Even the civilian tugboat captain trying to get *Minnesota* off the shoals asked "What can that little thing do?" He concluded, "We could lick her ourselves."

Around 7:30 A.M., *Virginia* returned and headed for *Minnesota*. Seeing her approach, *Monitor*'s crew prepared their ship for action. They battened down the hatches and placed stoppers in the deck skylights, removed the smokestacks and vent stacks, and keyed up the turret. Lieutenant Worden called to *Minnesota*'s captain, Gershon Van Brunt, "I will stand by you to the last if I can help you." Captain Van Brunt replied that *Monitor* could do nothing for him.

As they approached *Minnesota*, some on *Virginia* noticed a raftlike vessel with what looked like a boiler on its deck. The strange object contained no smokestack, suggesting that it had no engine. Lieutenant Eggleston aboard *Virginia* thought it "the strangest looking craft we had ever seen before." Lieutenant Jones, commanding *Virginia*, appears to have recognized that the "shingle" was the Union ironclad, but he chose to focus on *Minnesota*. At 8:30 A.M., *Virginia* opened fire on the grounded frigate with her bow pivot gun, and the two ships fired at each other over *Monitor*.

Squeezed into *Monitor*'s tiny pilothouse with the helmsman and the pilot, Lieutenant Worden ordered *Monitor* directly toward *Virginia* and placed his ship between the Confederate ironclad and *Minnesota*. Captain Van Brunt wrote in his report that *Monitor* "immediately ran down in my wake, right within the range of the *Merrimack*, completely covering my ship as far as was possible with her dimensions, and, much to my astonishment, laid herself right alongside of the *Merrimack*, and the contrast was that of a pigmy to a giant."

A Novel Idea

Monitor's most distinctive feature was her turret. In preparation for battle, the turret would be "keyed up" a few inches off the deck so that it could revolve. Supported on a central spindle, it could make a full 360-degree rotation in as little as twenty-four seconds. A wheel inside the turret controlled the motion.

This design allowed *Monitor* to fight more efficiently than a traditional warship carrying dozens of guns. An ordinary ship relied on the combined "weight of metal" of the broadside, and aimed the guns by moving the ship. But at any given time, half of the guns faced away from the enemy. *Monitor*'s revolving turret meant that the ship's orientation no longer mattered. Only the turret had to turn, and no guns were ever useless. *Monitor* carried two smoothbore 11-inch Dahlgren guns, which took six to eight minutes to load. She did not have a great volume of fire, but her guns were massive, making up in power what they lacked in quantity.

Unlike on other ships, *Monitor*'s commanding and executive officers were separated during battle. The commanding officer stood in the pilothouse, navigating the ship, while the executive officer directed the guns in the turret. Communication between the two relied on a speaking tube running between the turret and the pilothouse. ★

Inside *Monitor*'s turret, the men waited in suspense, wondering what would happen when *Virginia*'s shots finally struck their iron. The Confederate ironclad had destroyed the wooden ships that faced her the day before. What would happen to their own tiny ship?

Would their iron hold? Would *Virginia* ram and sink *Monitor* as she had *Cumberland*?

With the port stoppers closed, the turret was a dark and silent place. A little light filtered into the turret through the metal grating that formed the roof, supplementing a couple of lanterns. Acting Assistant Paymaster William Keeler remembered, "The most profound silence reigned," and the men stood like statues so that "if there had been a coward heart there its throb would have been audible, so *intense* was the stillness." They heard a gun thunder. Then another. Another. Then a broadside from *Minnesota*.

Inside the turret, the men worked in a deafening hell.

As soon as *Monitor* lay alongside *Virginia*, Worden stopped the engine and gave the order: "Commence firing!" Acting Master Louis Stodder turned the wheel controlling the turret, they lifted the port stopper and ran out the gun, and *Monitor* fired her first shot. Quartermaster Peter Truscott recalled, "You can see surprise on a ship just

the same as you can see it in a human being, and there was surprise all over the *Merrimac*."

The Confederate ironclad responded with a "rattling broadside." The crash of the projectiles against the turret's iron walls worried the men inside—until they realized that the shots did not penetrate. "A look of confidence passed over the men's faces," Lt. Samuel Dana Greene, commanding the guns, remembered, "and we believed the *Merrimac* would not repeat the work she had accomplished the day before."

The ironclads focused on each other, ranging so close that they collided at least five times.

Technical Difficulties

Both ships experienced technical difficulties during their first battle. The white marks placed on *Monitor*'s deck to orient the men in the turret were obliterated early in the action. Closed up in the revolving iron drum, Lieutenant Greene lost track of which way was which so that when word came from the pilothouse that *Virginia* was on, for example, the starboard beam, Greene did not even know where the starboard beam was.

In addition, the turret became difficult to start and stop. Not designed for sea travel, *Monitor* had nearly sunk on her way down from New York when a storm and rough seas hit her. Instead of letting the turret's weight form a watertight seal as Ericsson had intended, the Navy Yard had keyed up the turret and stuffed the gap underneath with bits of rope called "oakum." These washed out, resulting in a

waterfall 63 feet in circumference, right into the middle of the ship. By the time of the battle, the turret mechanism had begun to rust.

As the men worked their guns, they also realized that hauling open the port stoppers before each shot would prematurely exhaust them. They needed all their energy and strength to run the guns forward, so they left the stoppers open and protected themselves by turning the ports away from *Virginia* while reloading.

As a result of these difficulties, Lieutenant Greene wrote, "when a gun was ready for firing, the turret would be started on its revolving journey in search of the target, and when found, it was taken 'on the fly.'" Of course, Greene's view of the world consisted of only a few inches over the muzzles of the guns. Imagine what must have gone through Greene's head as he watched for *Virginia*'s bulk to appear in those few inches: he could not simply fire at any dark mass that appeared in his line of vision,

because it could be his own pilothouse. Nor could he fire at *Virginia* automatically every time she appeared—he had to make sure that she did not lie directly astern, such that he would fire his guns over *Monitor*'s boilers and damage them with the concussion of the blast. And always hovering in his mind was the knowledge that an enemy shell through one of the gun ports would kill the men in the turret, and *Monitor* did not have another gun crew on board.

Another issue came up with the speaking tube. Designed in such a way that it could only be used if the turret faced forward, it could not work as the turret revolved during battle. As a result, Paymaster Keeler and Clerk Daniel Toffey carried messages back and forth between the pilothouse and the turret. Though enthusiastic at their job, they were both landsmen. They did not know naval jargon, so, in Greene's words, "our technical communications sometimes miscarried."

Meanwhile, *Virginia* had troubles of her own. Being

the bigger ship was not necessarily a good thing. *Monitor*, with her smaller draft and sharper handling, could go places that *Virginia* could not, and ran circles around the Confederate ironclad. In contrast, *Virginia* handled like a waterlogged vessel and was as "unwieldy as Noah's ark" because her steering gear was insufficient for her weight of over 3,000 tons. Her turning circle covered about a mile and took the better part of an hour.

Water leaking into her hold further affected *Virginia*'s mobility, and her engines struggled. Originally condemned on USS *Merrimack*, the engines had then sat underwater for a month. Now, the riddled smokestack, which according to her surgeon "would have permitted a flock of crows to fly through it without inconvenience," could not draw enough fresh air to feed the engines properly. ★

Gun crews stripped to the waist and feverishly sponged, rammed, ran their guns forward, fired, then did it again. Inside the turret, the men worked in a deafening hell. Shots slammed against the iron walls, and the guns thundered and recoiled. Smoke hung in the air, and sweat dripped off powder-blackened bodies. Nuts blown off their bolts by the impact of enemy shells flew about the cramped space, bruising the men but fortunately not striking anyone in the eye with what would have been a fatal blow.

Like *Virginia*'s gun crews the day before, the men in the turret learned not to lean against the walls. At one point, a shell struck outside where Truscott, Stodder, and Chief Engineer Alban Stimers stood. The concussion knocked them all down, but their injuries depended on how they touched the wall. Stimers, resting his hand against it, fell, but popped right up again. Stodder, resting his knee against it, was blown clear across the turret, over both guns, and knocked unconscious for an hour. Truscott, standing with his head only inches from the point of impact, "dropped over like a dead man," he later recalled, and lay for some time in a semiconscious state.

Hull of *Virginia*

A little after 10:00 A.M., *Virginia*'s crew felt a shudder throughout their ship that must have made every heart sink. *Virginia* had run aground. *Monitor* took advantage of her own shallower draft and circled her stricken prey. Before long, the little ironclad settled in a position where the Confederate guns could not reach her, and pounded away at the immobile leviathan.

By this time, *Virginia* had used so much coal over two days of fighting that she rode high out of the water. With the eaves of her casemate ordinarily not more than 6 inches below the surface, a slight ripple could leave her bare at the waterline, except for a 1-inch layer of iron extending a couple of feet downward. Now, her eaves approached the surface, risking exposing her hull to the point that the ship was no longer an ironclad.

A terrifying shudder was felt throughout the ship. *Virginia* had run aground.

For nearly fifteen minutes, *Virginia*'s gun crews waited in excruciating inactivity. Beneath their feet, the ship quaked as her engines labored, but she did not move. The men heard enemy projectiles strike and crack their ship's iron. The casemate's wooden backing shifted inward several inches under the pounding. The end would come soon unless their ship started moving again. Given

enough time with a stationary target, *Monitor* might hit the same place twice to pierce *Virginia's* armor, or manage a shot at the waterline. But the gun crews could only stand idle and trust the men in the engine room below to save them.

In the engine room, Chief Engineer H. Ashton Ramsay's men lashed down the safety valves to raise as much steam as possible. Ramsay recalled how they "heaped quick-burning combustibles into the already raging fires, and brought the boilers to a pressure that would have been unsafe under ordinary circumstances." Safety no longer mattered; the alternatives were surrender or destruction.

Minute after minute passed, but the ship did not budge even as the pressure gauge went far past the danger point. The ship's propeller churned and churned. Ramsay continued, "We piled on oiled cotton waste, splints of wood, anything that would burn faster than coal. It seemed impossible that the boilers could stand the pressure we were crowding upon them." Ramsay had about reached the point of despair when, with "one Samsonian effort," *Virginia* "dragged herself off the shoal by main strength." The relieved gun crews let out a thunderous cheer.

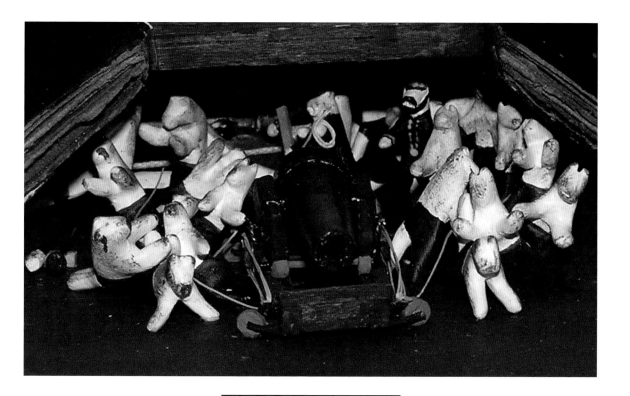

Seeing the ineffectiveness of guns against *Monitor*, Lieutenant Jones decided to ram her. After nearly an hour of maneuvering the unwieldy *Virginia*, he gave the order, "Go ahead, full steam!" Unfortunately for the Confederates, *Monitor* turned away and received only a glancing blow.

At the same time, Lieutenant Greene fired a shot at the forward part of *Virginia*'s casemate. He believed it would have penetrated *Virginia*'s armor if Navy Department regulations had allowed him to use thirty pounds of powder instead of a cautious fifteen.

Monitor fired at point-blank range, forcing *Virginia*'s iron inward.

Monitor traveled down *Virginia*'s port side and came up on her after quarter, her bow against *Virginia*'s side. Greene fired both guns at point-blank range.

The shells struck halfway up *Virginia*'s casemate, abreast of the after pivot gun, and forced the iron inward several inches. The concussion knocked over the crews of the after guns, leaving the men stunned and bleeding from the nose and ears.

After three hours of fighting, *Monitor* withdrew to shallows to replenish the turret's ammunition supply. Unable to reach her, *Virginia* returned to *Minnesota*, whose crew had watched the fight between the ironclads with interest, while returning occasional shots lobbed at them by the Confederate ironclad. One *Minnesota* man wrote about the fight, "It was really laughable. The *Merrimac* was making strenuous efforts to get down to us, but always just

before her was the diminutive 'Pill Box' waiting every chance and putting in a shot at each."

Monitor returned to the fight before *Virginia* could re-create much of the previous day's destruction against the frigate. Lieutenant Worden tried to ram *Virginia*'s stern to disable her propeller, but a steering malfunction made *Monitor* miss by a couple of feet. If *Monitor* had hit *Virginia*'s rudder and propeller, the battle would have been over.

As *Monitor* passed by, a shell from *Virginia*'s after pivot gun

"Save the Minnesota if you can," ordered a blind Lt. Worden.

struck her pilothouse at a range of 30 feet.

The explosion dislodged the iron logs sheltering the pilot-house and stunned Worden, who was looking through the

eye slit at the point of impact. Worden's left eye was permanently blinded and gunpowder under the skin caused a gray shadow on the side of his face for the rest of his life.

Not knowing how badly *Monitor* might be damaged, the blinded Worden ordered her to pull away and sent for Lieutenant Greene, who then took command. Even though seriously injured, Worden's first concern was their mission; he told his officers, "I cannot see, but do not mind me. Save the *Minnesota* if you can."

Small But Mighty

We have all heard the saying "Small but mighty." We tend to think of the fight between the ironclads as simply ending in a draw. Sure, *Monitor* was not destroyed by *Virginia*, but does that make her "mighty," or just durable?

On the morning of March 9, *Monitor* appeared small and weak. How could she—with only two guns—stand against the "horrid creation of a nightmare," when all the iron of the Union flotilla had no effect? Even though *Minnesota* was hobbled by being hard aground, surely the great frigate could do more against *Virginia* than the cheesebox could. As if to emphasize the point, the frigate and *Virginia* traded shots overtop *Monitor*.

Yet not only did *Monitor* survive the pounding of *Virginia*'s guns, she proactively engaged the Confederate ironclad and fulfilled her mission to save *Minnesota*. No matter how *Virginia* came at the grounded frigate, *Monitor* always blocked her path.

Monitor was small, but she proved herself mighty that day. In fact, Lieutenant Worden and his little ironclad proved their worth so well that the Union went on to build more of the curious-looking ironclads, confident now that the size of the vessel did not matter. ★

Greene found the pilothouse damaged but not destroyed and determined that the steering gear was still intact. He started *Monitor* back into the fight, but about twenty minutes had elapsed and *Virginia* was headed away, thinking *Monitor* had withdrawn. Greene interpreted this as a retreat and took up a position by *Minnesota* at about 12:30 P.M. Aboard *Virginia*, Lieutenant Jones was willing to renew the attack, but with the tide receding and *Virginia* experiencing leaks and engine trouble, he withdrew for repairs.

Due to the misunderstanding, both sides claimed victory, but it was *Monitor* that succeeded in her mission: to save *Minnesota*.

IN STARK CONTRAST TO THE CARNAGE AND DESTRUCTION OF THE day before, after hours of fighting, both ships suffered only a few wounded and a lot of dents. *Virginia* suffered some crushed ribs and beams and bent and broken plates.

At the end of the first day, an observer would have seen a single ship capable of picking off one Union ship after another until she pierced the blockade. The age of wood had ended. Once more ironclads joined *Virginia* in the task, the Northern stranglehold on Southern ports would fall to pieces. But at the end of the second day, an observer would have seen the odds evened, the threat met and stopped. It is no wonder, then, that both North and South hurried to make more ironclads, improving on their designs and never looking back. The age of iron had begun.

Chapter 4

The Gettysburg Campaign

IN JUNE 1863, THE CONFEDERATE ARMY OF NORTHERN VIRGINIA MARCHED INTO Pennsylvania. Gen. Robert E. Lee not only intended to take the fighting out of war-torn Virginia, but also hoped to win a victory in the North. If he could defeat the Union Army of the Potomac on its own soil, perhaps war-weary Northerners would clamor for peace.

On June 30, Confederate infantry under Brig. Gen. James Johnston Pettigrew approached Gettysburg, a small town at the center of a network of roads, from the northwest. At the same time, Union cavalrymen under Brig. Gen. John Buford rode into town from the south. Both sides saw each other, and

the Confederates withdrew, obeying Lee's orders to avoid a general engagement while the army was scattered. That night, Pettigrew tried to warn his superiors, but they believed the Union army was nowhere near.

Meanwhile, Buford recognized that the hills and ridges around Gettysburg would give the Union army a solid position to fight from. But he must hold off the Confederates long enough for the Union infantry to arrive. He sent word of the situation to Maj. Gen. John Reynolds of the I Corps—the closest infantry—and prepared to defend the town.

At 7:30 A.M. on July 1, northwest of town, Lt. Marcellus Jones borrowed the carbine of

a Union cavalry sergeant beside him, took aim, and fired the first shot of the battle. Buford's men fought dismounted, kneeling and firing like infantry.

If Lee defeated the Union army here, would the North ask for peace?

As more and more Confederates arrived, seriously outnumbering them, Buford's men relied on their carbines to make up the difference. Designed for use on

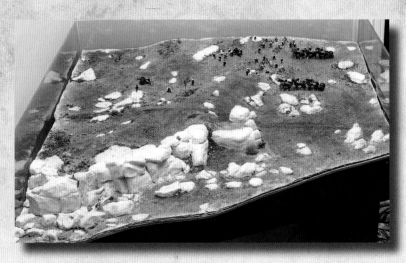

"Give Them Shell!"

Scale: 1:96

Number of Cats:
US: 50

Dimensions:
3'1" x 3'4"

Date Created:
Oct. 17, 2008–April 12, 2009

Gen. John Buford

horseback, carbines were shorter than ordinary rifles and, more importantly, they were breech-loaders, meaning that cavalry-men could reload more quickly since they did not have to ram the cartridge down the barrel.

Just as the situation grew desperate for the cavalry-men, Union infantry arrived. A bullet killed Reynolds while he urged his men for-ward, but his corps held their ground, buying time for more troops to reach the field.

Neither army was prepared for a battle, and it became a race between two spread-out armies, with Confederates coming in from the northwest and north, and Union troops coming up from the south. As the afternoon wore on, the Confederates overwhelmed the Union line. Fleeing sol-diers filled the town, crowding into the streets and alleys.

Thousands were captured. Those who escaped came to Cemetery Hill south of town, where reserve units waited and officers worked to rally the men. With evening coming on, time still remained for the Confed-erates to press their advantage, but inexplicably they halted.

By evening, the Union posi-tion had taken on the shape that would become known as the "fishhook." The line began on the right with the "hook" curving from east to west across Culp's and Cem-etery Hills. It then ran south down Cemetery Ridge, forming the "shank" of the fishhook,

The Children of the Battlefield

Covering the Union retreat on July 1, the 154th New York (XI Corps) fought in a brickyard in the northern part of town until nearly surrounded. When the regiment finally pulled back, a sergeant, shot above the heart, fell near the intersection of Stratton and York Streets. Collapsed against a pump, he pulled a small photo from his pocket and gazed at the faces of his three young children. After the battle, that photograph became the only way to identify him.

Dr. John Bourns, a volunteer surgeon, made it his mission to find the fallen soldier's family. He led efforts to distribute copies of the photo throughout the North. All proceeds from sales of the photo—as well as related poetry and songs—were set aside in a fund to be given to the family.

One publication that ran an article was the *American Presbyterian*. In the town of Portville, New York, only one person subscribed to the paper, but that reader showed the article to Philinda Humiston,

thinking it might apply to her children. At Philinda's request, Dr. Bourns sent a copy of the photo, and she immediately recognized her children—Frank, Frederick, and Alice. At last, Sgt. Amos Humiston was identified.

After the war, in 1866, the Soldiers' Orphans' National Homestead opened in Gettysburg. Philinda served as the first matron until 1869, when she remarried and moved

to Massachusetts. The orphanage was growing, so to provide more space, a second building was built in 1869 as a girls' dormitory. Even though the orphanage closed in 1877, the buildings remained, and in 1903, the dormitory was moved up to the street. Civil War Tails Museum currently resides in the old dormitory. The original orphanage building stands north of us. ★

A Subtle Witness

In 1862, Union general Philip Kearny designed badges for the men of his division to wear. The red diamonds became known as the "Kearny Patch," and soon the entire corps wore them. In early 1863, badges were instituted throughout the Army of the Potomac. Each corps received a different shape: a circle for the I Corps, trefoil (clover leaf or club) for the II, diamond for the III, Maltese cross for the V, Greek cross for the VI, crescent moon for the XI, and star for the XII. In addition, each division within the corps had a different color: red for the 1st division, white for the 2nd, and blue for the 3rd. So, by looking at a soldier's hat, one could tell which corps and division he belonged to.

Soldiers were proud of their corps badges, and on the Union regimental monuments at Gettysburg, you can see all the various shapes. Most areas of the battlefield have one corps badge present

Maltese cross (V Corps) corps badges

(Cemetery Ridge, for example, has mostly trefoils on the monuments), but a drive through the Wheatfield area will show the III Corps diamond, the II Corps trefoil, and the V Corps Maltese cross, all mingled together.

The monuments stand as silent sentinels now, and the fields and woods lie peaceful with only rainwater, not blood,

making the ground soggy. But pause a moment and ponder just what it means that you see more than only III Corps diamonds around you. The variety in corps badge shapes bears a subtle witness to the chaotic battle and the desperation with which Union generals threw every unit they could find into the fighting there on July 2. ★

and ended just short of two hills, Little Round Top and Big Round Top, on the Union left. To the north and west, the

Confederate line mirrored the Union line, stretching through town and running southward along Seminary Ridge.

Despite having been in command of the Union army for only three days, Maj. Gen. George G. Meade found himself in a good position. His men held the high ground. The Confederates would have to come, climbing, to them. But Union army commanders had botched advantages before; only time would tell if Meade was the general that the army needed in order to win, or if he would be just another failure.

On July 2, on the left flank of the Union line, Maj. Gen. Daniel Sickles moved his III Corps forward to higher ground—three-quarters of a mile away from the rest of the Union army. To make matters worse, at the Peach Orchard, the middle of his corps bent at a right angle. When Lt. Gen. James Longstreet's Confederate corps attacked that afternoon, they approached the men in the orchard from two directions.

By the time General Meade realized Sickles's blunder, there was no time to move the corps. Reinforcements from all along the Union line hurried to Sickles's aid, but with Confederates sweeping down on both left and right, the III Corps collapsed. Meade sent more and more men to plug the gap where Sickles should have been south of Cemetery Ridge, until most of the army faced Longstreet. By nightfall, the Confederates had taken the Peach Orchard,

Was General Meade the leader the Union needed, or just another failure?

the Wheatfield, and Devil's Den, but the left flank of the Union army remained intact.

As evening fell, Confederates hit East Cemetery Hill and Culp's Hill on the Union right. Union reinforcements reached East Cemetery Hill in time to stop the Confederate breakthrough. On Culp's Hill, Confederates took some trenches (left empty when the troops reinforced Sickles), but lack of support prevented them from pressing on. As the desperate fighting died down around 9:30 P.M., Union men remained in control of the two hills.

ONE OF THE STRANGEST FEATURES OF THE GETTYSBURG BATTLE-field is Devil's Den, a haphazard pile of massive boulders on the end of a ridge. The rocks are part of an enormous sheet of igneous

Infantry stood on the left of the Union line at Devil's Den. Capt. James E. Smith's 4th New York Light Artillery was ordered to join them.

Devil's Den was not designed for artillery. The steep slope and boulders made the ascent too difficult for horses to haul up the guns and limbers. The fact that the ridge contained a reasonable field of fire for artillery meant nothing if the guns could not get there. But

rock that lies beneath the battle-field, but to one ignorant of geological causes, Devil's Den remains a haunting place that, in the words of a veteran, "seems cursed of God and abandoned of man."

Before the battle of Gettys-burg, the local farmers saw no use for the "Big Rocks." They could never imagine that thousands of men would fight for the useless ridge and pay for it with their blood.

On the morning of July 2, the 124th New York Infan-try, nicknamed the "Orange Blossoms," and the 4th Maine

Artillerymen manhandled each Union cannon up the rocky slope in the July heat.

orders were orders. So Smith's artillerymen unlimbered their guns and, for the next hour, they manhandled each one up the slope, sweating in the July heat, pulling on ropes and shoving with their shoulders to the wheels and axles.

One by one, the Parrott rifled guns reached the crest. Captain Smith found that only four guns would fit, so he placed the remaining two Parrotts behind

them in the valley between Devil's Den and Little Round Top to protect the left flank.

Since the limbers could not fit on the crest, the artillerymen piled ammunition next to their guns. They would count on runners to replenish the supply during the coming fight. The work must have made each man cringe, as they knew what would happen if a Rebel shot hit one of the piles.

The battery engaged enemy artillery in a duel that lasted for about half an hour. Then, Confederate infantry advanced. A soldier of the 124th New York recalled that the Parrotts' fire "tore gap after gap throughout the ranks of the Confederate foe." But the gray line stretched far past the battery's left, worrying Smith, so he asked the 4th Maine to join the two guns in the valley. This left him with no infantry support behind him, but he hoped his Parrotts could hold their own.

As the Confederates drew closer and closer, the battery

ran low on the case shot that was most effective against advancing infantry. Told of the shortage, Smith ordered, "Give them shell! give them solid shot! Damn them, give them anything!" The Parrotts continued firing, probably using canister, which lost its effectiveness when used in a rifled gun. Whereas a smoothbore cannon scattered the little iron balls like a shotgun, a rifled gun sent them in a narrow spiral pattern. But the gun crews had no choice.

Meanwhile, on the battery's right, the 124th New York, led by Col. Augustus Van Horne Ellis and Maj. James Cromwell, charged the Confederates. Seeing Cromwell fall dead from his horse, Ellis shouted, "My God, men! Your major's down; save

him! save him!" The "Orange Blossoms" charged again, turned wild by the sight of their beloved major falling. Moments later, Ellis also fell dead.

Confederates infiltrated the boulders of Devil's Den and began picking off artillerymen. Unable to depress their cannon barrels low enough to fire on the Confederates, Smith's men could only fire at Brig. Gen. Henry Benning's fresh brigade now emerging from the distant trees. Smith, seeing his men fall, knew he needed infantry help. He ran over to the 124th New York with tears in his eyes, begging, "For God's sake, men, don't let them take my guns away from me!" But by then the situation was desperate for the "Orange Blossoms" as well,

Orange Blossoms?

Perhaps this is not the nickname you would pick for your hard-fighting regiment. So where did it come from? Most of the men in the 124th New York came from Orange County, New York. Colonel Ellis was a tough, hard-swearing former sea captain, but the men in his regiment respected him, and he affectionately called them his "Orange Blossoms." If you go to the battlefield, you can see a statue of Colonel Ellis standing on the top of the 124th's monument, looking over the field where he and many of his brave men fell that day. ★

and with Confederates flanking them on the left near Smith's guns, they were forced to retreat.

Knowing he had no time to pull his guns off the ridge, Smith ordered his men to leave the guns behind but take the rammers and other implements. The Confederates, when they reached the guns, found they could not turn them on the Union troops because they had no equipment with which to work the guns.

Union reinforcements managed to retake the ridge, but Benning's brigade arrived and reclaimed Devil's Den for good.

That night, the Confederates snuck Smith's guns off the ridge, wrapping the wheels in blankets so they made no sound.

4639

"At All Hazards"

Scale: 1:36

Number of Cats:
US: 48

Dimensions:
2'8.5" x 2'9.5"

Date Created:
2003

AS THE UNION LINE NEAR THE WHEATFIELD CRUMBLED, CAPT. John Bigelow's 9th Massachusetts Light Artillery withdrew to the Trostle farmyard. The battery had had their first taste of battle that afternoon and now hoped to reach safety before the Confederate infantry overtook them. Just then, Bigelow's commander, Lt. Col. Freeman McGilvery, galloped up, his horse streaming blood from four wounds.

"Captain Bigelow," he shouted, "there is not an infantryman back of you along the whole line . . . you must remain where you are and hold your position at all hazards, and sacrifice your battery, if need be, until at least I can find some batteries to put in position. . . . The enemy are coming down on you now."

Faced with what he considered a "superhuman" task, Bigelow placed his six guns in an arc inside the angle of a stone wall. About 50 yards ahead of them, the ground rose, blocking their view.

At first, Bigelow's men ricocheted solid shot off the rise into the unseen Confederates, but since hitting anything that way depended on luck, they finally loaded the guns with double canister and waited. When infantry appeared over the rise, the guns opened fire and continued firing as quickly as the men could reload them.

As the two guns of the left section fired, their recoil brought them closer and closer to the wall, until the crews ran out of space. Bigelow ordered them to the rear, while the other four continued to fire canister. The first gun's team of horses galloped through a gate and wheeled into Trostle's Lane.

"Hold your position at all hazards . . . sacrifice your battery, if need be," shouted McGilvery.

But the cannon overturned, blocking the gate. The only way for the second gun to escape was to go over the wall. The horses could easily jump it, but could the cannon and limber? The artillerymen knew they had to try. They took away some of the rocks to make a gap, then galloped the horses through. The limber and cannon bounded and crashed after them but successfully made it over the rocks.

Bigelow asked his men to enlarge the gap for the remaining guns. As he watched the men work, Confederates on the battery's flank fired and wounded him twice.

By now, Bigelow remembered, "the enemy crowded to the very

Heavier Than They Look

A gun's weight depended on its type. The barrel of a 12-pounder Napoleon, a common smoothbore in the field artillery, weighed 1,227 pounds. The gun carriage (wheels, and so on) weighed 1,128 pounds. The limber weighed 880 pounds—empty. When you add it all up, plus the implements and ammunition, the horses of a 12-pounder Napoleon would be pulling about 3,875 pounds! ★

muzzles of [the guns], but were blown away by the canister . . . Sergeant after sergt. was struck down, horses were plunging and laying all around, bullets now came in on all sides . . . The air was dark with smoke." Bigelow ordered his men to fall back, abandoning the four guns.

Bugler Charles Reed led the wounded captain from the field, controlling both of their horses with one hand, while supporting Bigelow with his other hand. Because of the severity of Bigelow's wounds, Reed kept the horses at a walk. As they crossed in front of the 6th Maine Battery, sent up by McGilvery, an officer rode out to hurry them up, since the cannons were

ready to fire. Bigelow replied that they could not go faster, but the battery should fire anyway. He and Reed would take their chances. The guns fired, sending canister and shell shrieking past the two men. Amazingly, Bigelow and Reed passed through, unharmed. Thanks to Reed's efforts, Capt. Bigelow survived. In 1895, Charles Reed received the Medal of Honor for his actions.

Capt. John Bigelow (black horse) and Bugler Charles Reed (bay horse)

"The Boys Are Still There"

Scale: 1:96

Number of Cats: US: 1,053; CS: 574

Dimensions: 11'2" x 4'10"

Date Created: 2012 (still under construction)

A S THE FIGHTING DEVELOPED AROUND THE PEACH ORCHARD, Wheatfield, and Devil's Den, Brig. Gen. Gouverneur K. Warren climbed Little Round Top and was shocked to find only a signal station there. The small rocky hill sat at the left end

A Signal Corps station

of the Union line, and it was a straight shot all the way up the Union line on Cemetery Ridge. If Confederates managed to haul artillery up there, they could enfilade—that is, shoot along the length of—the entire Union line, and maybe destroy the Union army.

Three men and a signal flag stood in their way. Warren scrambled to find troops. One staff officer found Col. Strong Vincent and his brigade awaiting orders on their way to reinforce Sickles. After hearing the situation, Vincent declared that he would take the responsibility for ignoring his original orders and leading his brigade to the hill instead.

Once in position, Vincent's four regiments formed a line that began with the 20th Maine on a small wooded spur on the hill's southern slope. To their right, the 83rd Pennsylvania's line curved westward through the trees. The 44th New York continued the line, and the 16th Michigan

anchored the brigade's right flank on a "shelf" partway down the cleared western hillside.

As Colonel Vincent showed Col. Joshua Lawrence Chamberlain where he wanted the 20th Maine, he told the former college professor, "I place you here! This is the left of the Union line. You understand. You are to hold this ground at all costs!" As the Maine men settled down among the boulders, Colonel Chamberlain sent Company B out as skirmishers to the front and left. Skirmishers acted as an "early warning" system; when the men in the regiment heard them firing, they knew the enemy was near. Company B moved down the slope, seeking to join up

with the 16th Michigan's skirmishers on their left—only they never found any skirmishers, since the Michiganders had moved to the brigade's right flank. But they kept going through the trees, looking.

Vincent's men were hardly in position when Confederates appeared. The 4th and 5th Texas struggled up the open western slope, clambering over massive boulders, and struck the 44th New York first. The 4th Alabama

Only minutes after Vincent's brigade took position, Confederates appeared.

then struck the 83rd Pennsylvania in Vincent's center. Not seeing any Confederates to their front, the 20th Maine fired to their right at the Alabamians. Then, the 4th Texas hit the 16th Michigan. Vincent's brigade was now fully engaged.

On top of Big Round Top, just south of Little Round Top, Col. William Oates and his 15th Alabama sat resting with

the 47th Alabama. They had climbed the big hill in pursuit of pesky sharpshooters, and now the men sat amidst the boulders, wiping sweat from their faces and wishing for their canteens. Earlier that afternoon, a detail of men had taken the 15th Alabama's canteens to refill them. They had not yet returned when the order came to advance. Now, after climbing the steep, rocky, wooded slope, a drink of water sounded awfully good.

Caught in the hail of crossfire, the tiny 47th Alabama was chewed to pieces.

Oates thought Big Round Top an ideal place for artillery, despite the heavy woods and boulders. But as the fighting developed below him, he set aside his wishes and led the two regiments down into the fray. As they started up the smaller hill, they met a storm of musketry from Yankees hidden among the boulders above them.

The tiny 47th Alabama, caught in a crossfire between the 83rd Pennsylvania's left and the 20th Maine's right, was chewed to pieces.

Col. William Oates

Lt. Col. Michael Bulger

Seeing the men of his 47th Alabama fall around him, Lt. Col. Michael Bulger tried to lead them forward in one last charge. Partway between the two lines, a bullet struck him in the lung.

He staggered to the ground behind a tree and remained there for the rest of the fight, stranded between the lines, his sword and pistol in his lap, and blood running from his mouth. Maj. James Campbell tried to rally the 47th, but the shattered regiment was finished.

After the fighting ended, Bulger was captured. Despite the severity of his wound, he survived the war and lived to the age of 95. ★

Lt. Col. Michael Bulger

MEANWHILE, TWO ARTILLERY OFFICERS RODE UP TO GENeral Warren, who still waited on the crest of Little Round Top, apparently unaware of the presence of Vincent's brigade. Capt. Augustus Martin, commanding the V Corps artillery, and Lt. Charles Hazlett, commanding Battery D, 5th U.S. Artillery, had appreciated the hill's importance when they first saw it. Already, Hazlett had started his battery up the hill.

Martin and Hazlett found the crest narrow and rocky, with little space to work the guns—if the six Parrotts could even get up the slope through the trees and boulders. If the artillerymen succeeded in placing the guns, the slope in front was so steep that, as at Devil's Den, they could never reach the Confederates in front of them. The battery could only fire across the small valley to Devil's Den.

Warren told Hazlett that the hill was "no place for efficient artillery fire."

Unfazed, Charlie Hazlett replied, "Never mind that, the sound of my guns will be encouraging to our troops and disheartening to the others, and my battery's of no use if this hill is lost."

Hazlett's guns started up the back slope of Little Round Top at a trot. Lt. Benjamin Rittenhouse recalled "each man and horse trying to pull the whole battery by himself," until the steep slope forced the horses to halt. Engineers cut down trees to open a road, and the artillerymen began the monumental task of wrestling their cannons up the slope by hand. It would take them over an hour in the oppressive heat and humidity. Some men hauled on ropes, while others leaned their shoulders against the axles.

"I have since wondered how we ever got our guns up that hill."

Sweat stung their eyes, and their hands grew slick, as the men gripped the wheels' spokes and strained to move the guns, inch by inch. On every side, boulders loomed, and smaller rocks seemed eager to trip a man or block a wheel. One artilleryman wrote later, "I have since wondered how we ever got our guns up that hill."

On the spur, using the trees to screen their activities, Oates moved his 15th Alabama around the 20th Maine's left flank to get at their rear.

But Chamberlain's officers noticed the movement, and Chamberlain stretched his line to one rank instead of two and "refused" his line, bending the regiment into almost a right angle.

The Confederates struck Vincent's entire line a second time, and the fighting raged for over an hour, seesawing up and down the slope. Pvt. Elisha Coan of the 20th Maine wrote, "The calm of the early afternoon had been succeeded by a cyclone."

The roar of musketry drowned out officers' shouted orders. Confederate lines attacked and withdrew. The firing erupted and died away and erupted again. Every time an attack subsided, more

To Love Your Enemy

Would you risk your life to save another's? What if the person is not a friend but an enemy?

In the center of Vincent's brigade, Pvt. Philip Grine of the 83rd Pennsylvania couldn't help but notice the wounded Confederates stranded between the two firing lines. During a lull in the fighting, he left the protection of his regiment and ventured down the slope to a wounded man. He carried the Confederate back up the hill and gave him to other Yankees to take to the aid station in the rear.

But one was not enough. Later in the fighting, Grine fetched a second injured Confederate. Exhausted after fighting hard and carrying two men, he asked a few others to help him retrieve a third man. When the Confederates began firing at them, the others scurried back to their lines. Undaunted, Grine continued on his mission. He did not return. After the fighting ended, the men of the 83rd found him lying dead

Pvt. Philip Grine

beside the Confederate he had gone to help.

Grine looked past the outward circumstances—the color of the uniform, the fact that they had just been trying to kill him—and he saw fellow men, just as worthy of living as he. Perhaps that is what it really means to "love your enemy"—to see him as a fellow human, and to value that life. Grine paid the ultimate

price for his beliefs, but his actions give us a beautiful picture of what it means to "love your neighbor as yourself."

No matter what you believe, perhaps we can all agree on one thing—the world would be a better place if we had the compassion of Philip Grine and valued all human life more than our own . . . and if we were willing to *do* something to preserve it, no matter the cost. ★

20th Maine's color guard

and more wounded were left stranded between the lines.

In the center of the 20th Maine, the color guard kept the Stars and Stripes flying proudly, even as Oates's men broke through the line again and again.

Typically made of sergeants and corporals, the color guard defended the flag and picked it up if the color sergeant fell. Here, the color sergeant Andrew Tozier stood with three corporals and, surprisingly, a private. Cpl. Melville Day fell dead with five bullets in him. A bullet struck Cpl. Charlie Reed in the wrist, but he refused to leave the field and traded Tozier his rifle for the flag. So far, Cpl. William Livermore and Private Coan remained unharmed.

Each time the Confederates fell back, the men of the 20th Maine gathered ammunition from the dead and wounded and settled behind the rocks and trees. On the regiment's right, they piled logs and rocks for more shelter.

Stretcher bearers retrieved wounded—Union and Confederate alike—to take back to the aid station and, eventually, the field hospital.

Meanwhile, Hazlett's men still wrestled their guns to the crest. Even with the help of nearby infantrymen, progress was slow. Gen. Warren even lent a hand. Later he would recall of Hazlett: "There he sat on his horse on the summit of the hill, with whole-souled animation encouraging our men, and pointing with his sword toward the enemy amidst a storm of bullets—a figure of intense admiration to me . . . No nobler man fought or fell that day than he."

20th Maine's aid station

From his horse on the summit, Hazlett rallied his men "with whole-souled animation."

Discoveries

After placing the rocks on our diorama, we saw only one plausible path through the boulders up which Hazlett could have brought his guns. Using an artilleryman's recollection that they turned left onto the crest, we placed our miniature guns on the crest to the left of our path and spaced them the correct 14 yards apart. We put the farthest gun as close to the infantry as the rocks allow, since some men of the 140th New York lost their hearing on account of Hazlett's guns firing over them.

This strung out our cannons almost to the location of the castlelike New York monument, much farther along the crest than the present-day cannons marking Hazlett's position. Interestingly, an old photo shows a memorial gun barrel placed about halfway between the current guns and the New York monument, signifying that one of Hazlett's had been placed there.

Comparing the boulder in the photo with our diorama, we discovered that we had placed one of our miniature cannons in nearly the same spot as the memorial gun barrel! While that memorial was taken away in subsequent years, it seems that whoever put it there knew what they were doing. ★

Knowing he still needed more men on the hill, Warren mounted his gray horse and rode off to find some. He and his aide, Lt. W. A. Roebling (who would later design the Brooklyn Bridge), saw the end of a column of infantry heading to the Peach Orchard area—Brig. Gen. Stephen Weed's brigade. Warren galloped up to the last regiment in the column, Col. Patrick O'Rorke's 140th New York. O'Rorke immediately turned his regiment to the hill, following Roebling. Warren rode off to report to General Meade, finally confident that Little Round Top was secure.

But, Oates's Alabamians attacked the 20th Maine's left

This attack could break the 20th Maine's thin line once and for all.

again, threatening to break the thin line once and for all. Colonel Chamberlain tried taking two companies from his right wing, but it caused so much confusion, he changed his mind, deciding not to start a rout.

In the center, the two companies on either side of the flag were decimated. Company A, to the left, had fewer than a dozen men remaining; Company F, to the right, was not much better off. Nearby, a tree, 3 to 4 inches in diameter, crashed to the ground, cut down by bullets.

Just Chance?

Colonel Chamberlain didn't know how close he came to dying on Little Round Top. One Confederate took aim, but just as he fired, a Union private moved between him and the colonel and was hit by the bullet. Another Confederate tried, but, he told Chamberlain after the war, as he began to squeeze the trigger, a "queer notion" came over him and made him stop. He shook off the feeling and tried again, but for the second time the feeling came over him. He gave up and picked another target.

What would have happened if Colonel Chamberlain had been shot? Would the 20th Maine have broken, allowing the exhausted Confederates to take the hill? Would the Confederates have captured Hazlett's battery and pounded the Union line, helping Longstreet's corps destroy the Union army?

Every battle contains moments when the smallest, seemingly "unimportant" detail makes a huge difference. Countless moments at Gettysburg combined into a Union victory that would affect the course of the war, and perhaps the world. Where would we be today if the United States were two nations during World War II? Would the Union or the Confederacy alone have had the resources to build the supply ships that overwhelmed Hitler's submarines by their sheer numbers? Or the men to send to the Normandy beaches on D-Day? Could two small nations have accomplished the work of one great nation? ★

On Vincent's right, the 4th and 5th Texas attacked a third time, now joined by the 48th Alabama on their left.

Evening was fast approaching and discipline was breaking down in the Texas regiments—some men fell back instead of advancing—but Vincent's battered brigade was low on ammunition, and the 48th Alabama overlapped the tiny 16th Michigan's flank. One more attack just might break the blue line.

Evening was falling, but one more charge might finally break the Union line.

As the Confederates struck Vincent's line, the 16th Michigan reeled. Half of the regiment, including the color guard and commander, fell back because of muddled orders, and half remained in line with the 44th New York. Vincent rushed among the retreating men, trying to rally them, as Chamberlain wrote, "by sheer force of his superb personality," but a bullet struck him and he fell, mortally wounded.

Twins at Gettysburg

A set of twins advanced with the 5th Texas. As they came within 20 yards of the Union lines, one of the brothers was hit. His twin caught him and lowered him to the ground, and then a bullet struck the second brother and he, too, fell dead.

Similarly, on the first day of battle, the 26th North Carolina marched into battle with three sets of twins in its ranks. By nightfall, five of the six men lay dead or mortally wounded.

As twins, we cannot imagine the anguish of losing our "other half." What horror must the twin of the 5th Texas have felt at seeing his brother fall dead? And what must that last twin of the 26th North Carolina have felt on the night of July 1, knowing that he was the only one remaining *out of six*? ★

Ordinary Becomes Extraordinary

Andrew Tozier was just an ordinary fellow from Maine. He had a hard life growing up with an abusive, alcoholic father and ran away to become a sailor. After he enlisted in the Union army in 1861, his life did not get any easier. He was wounded three times, captured, and spent time in two Confederate prisons. But on July 2, 1863, this ordinary man became an extraordinary soldier, worthy of the highest decoration a soldier can receive: the Medal of Honor.

After an hour of fighting on Little Round Top, only two men of the color guard remained unhurt near Tozier, but they were so shrouded in smoke that he seemed alone. Colonel Chamberlain

Sgt. Andrew Tozier

AUTHORS' COLLECTION

later wrote, "in the center, wreathed in battle smoke, stood the Color-Sergeant, Andrew Tozier. His color-staff planted in the ground at his side, the upper part clasped in his elbow, so holding the flag

upright, with musket and cartridges seized from the fallen comrade at his side, he was defending his sacred trust."

Tozier stood as firm as the boulder on which the regiment's monument stands today. Some say he stood on that very boulder, and that is why the veterans chose to place the memorial there.

In 1898, Andrew Tozier received the Medal of Honor for his bravery. He did not receive it because he was born a superhero or a superpatriot. Rather, he saw his duty and the security of his comrades as *so important* that he risked his own life to go above and beyond what was expected of him—and that made him a hero. ★

On the spur, the 20th Maine's Company A was gone; Company F, a mere shadow. Corporal Reed of the color guard, finally weakened by his wound, had gone to the rear. Coan and Livermore did their best to cover the gap around Tozier.

At long last, Hazlett's #2 gun opened fire on the Confederates

"No military music ever sounded sweeter . . ."

in Devil's Den. Capt. Eugene Nash of the 44th New York recalled, "No military music ever sounded sweeter and no aid was ever better appreciated." During the next lull, the 44th New York gave a cheer for the artillery. Hazlett had been right. Impractical though his guns might be in an objective sense,

The 15th Alabama broke through the Union's left wing, seizing the crest of the spur.

Lt. John Oates

Lt. John Oates suffered from a fever on July 2. He had had trouble keeping up on the march, and as the 15th Alabama prepared to attack, his brother and colonel, William, told him to remain behind. He was in no condition to advance with the regiment.

"No, brother," he replied. "Were I to do that it would be said that I avoided the battle and acted the coward. No sir!"

Lt. John Oates

Colonel Oates would never forget that moment.

Within a few hours, John lay mortally wounded. He was captured and taken to the V Corps hospital. On July 25, as he lay dying, he asked the ladies caring for him, "Tell my folks at home that I died in the arms of friends."

William Oates wrote that he had lost his "dearest relative on earth." ★

---

their presence on the hill was psychologically necessary.

The situation of the 44th New York and the remnants of the 16th Michigan grew desperate as the Confederates pressed closer and closer. The 48th Alabama stretched far beyond the 16th Michigan's right. Suddenly, boiling over the crest came the 140th New York, following "Paddy" O'Rorke. Seeing that his regiment had no time to form a proper battle line, O'Rorke drew his sword, called out, "Down this way, boys!" and dashed down the slope. Companies A and G followed him, scattering among the boulders to the 16th Michigan's right. O'Rorke

shouted, "Here they are men, commence firing!" and the two companies opened fire. The Confederates answered with a withering volley, and O'Rorke fell with a bullet in his neck. He bled to death within minutes.

On the spur, the 15th Alabama hit the 20th Maine yet again. The Mainers reeled and the Alabamians broke through. Colonel Chamberlain sent his brother, Tom, to get men and plug a gap near the flag. Lieutenant Chamberlain managed to pull the center back, closing the hole. Capt. Ellis Spear, commanding the left wing, and Capt. Joe Land used both hands on the flats of their swords to

literally hold their men in place. But Confederates led by Colonel Oates's brother John seized the crest of the spur. Hand-to-hand fighting broke out. A dozen feet to the right of Colonel Oates, John fell, wounded by over half a dozen bullets. Lieutenant Parks dragged him behind a boulder, where yet another bullet took off his finger.

The 20th Maine held their ground, the two wings bent nearly back to back, and the 15th Alabama fell back once more. During the lull, Chamberlain assessed his regiment. The right wing was low on ammunition and

about half of the left wing had fallen dead or wounded.

Behind him, he heard a "great roar of musketry" and, not knowing of the arrival of O'Rorke's 140th New York, he feared that the brigade's right had broken. Remembering Vincent's words, he knew he could not retreat. He also knew his men could not hold off another attack. He saw no alternative but to charge. He could not have known that the Confederates were exhausted, having marched all day, climbed and descended Big Round Top, and fought hard through the July heat—all without canteens of water. Colonel Oates had just decided to order a retreat.

Chamberlain thought he saw the Confederates gathering for another attack. Then, Lt. Holman Melcher asked if he could move Company F forward, so their wounded would be inside their lines, instead of stranded in the midst of the fighting. Chamberlain approved the request, adding that he was about to order a charge.

Capt. Ellis Spear

As Melcher returned to Company F, Chamberlain ordered, "Bayonet!" Only the right wing heard him and fixed bayonets.

Over on the left, the men had no idea what was going on. But they saw their flag moving forward, still carried by Sergeant Tozier, and Captain Spear ordered them forward, to maintain contact with the colors. When a regiment's flag advanced, the entire line advanced, and when it retreated, the men retreated. Receiving the order to advance and seeing their colors moving, the left wing knew it could only mean one thing.

They charged. As the left wing swung down the slope, the right wing joined them, and the entire regiment pivoted on the far-right companies.

Oates gave the word to retreat and, he said later, "we ran like a herd of wild cattle." Suddenly, to the rear of the Confederates, the 20th Maine's lost Company B appeared, taking the retreating troops by surprise and adding to the confusion and chaos.

As Colonel Chamberlain charged down the slope, he came upon Lt. Robert Wicker. The Confederate waited until Chamberlain was six feet away before firing his big Navy revolver in the colonel's face. The shot missed. Chamberlain knocked the revolver aside with his sword and lifted the sword's point to Wicker's neck. The lieutenant surrendered.

On Vincent's right, the 140th New York's arrival broke the Confederate attack. As the sun slipped behind the distant Blue Ridge Mountains, the Confederates retreated. But snipers' bullets from Devil's Den still searched out the crest of Little Round Top. General Weed had directed the rest of his brigade into position alongside the 140th New York, and now, as the firing died away and he watched the III Corps falling back from the Wheatfield, he was hit and fell, paralyzed from the shoulders down. Hazlett knelt over him for his last words and was struck in the head. Hazlett remained conscious but unable to speak. Both officers died that night.

On July 3, Colonel Vincent's orderly, Pvt. Oliver Norton, visited the colonel at the field hospital and found him pale and unable to speak because of the pain. But Norton could read the question in his eyes—*What happened? Did the men hold their ground?*

Lt. Robert Wicker

If Ever I Shook Hands Heartily...

When the 20th Maine found themselves without a surgeon, Colonel Chamberlain asked for his brother John, serving with the Christian Commission, to join the regiment. On July 2, John began the climb up Little Round Top with his brothers Joshua (Lawrence) and Thomas, but a solid shot passed close by the three of them, prompting Joshua to say, "Boys, I don't like this. Another such shot might make it hard for mother." Joshua sent Tom to the rear to hurry on the regiment and John up ahead to set up the regimental aid station and prepare for the wounded.

As the fighting raged, John could only wonder what had become of his brothers, since enemy soldiers targeted officers and especially the colonel of a regiment. After the battle, he finally found his brothers and recalled, "If ever I shook hands heartily, I did so then, as I looked on Lawrence and Thomas alive." ★

John Chamberlain

Thomas (left) and Joshua Lawrence Chamberlain

Norton gave a simple reply that spoke volumes, bringing Vincent the relief he so desperately needed: "The boys are still there, Colonel."

IF CONFEDERATES HAD TAKEN LITTLE ROUND TOP, COULD THEY HAVE destroyed the Union army? General Warren was not the only Union soldier to think so. Brig. Gen. John Geary of the XII Corps said that Confederates on the hill would have had "an opportunity of enfilading our entire left wing and center with a fire which could not fail to dislodge us."

If Longstreet's men had taken Little Round Top before Vincent arrived (Longstreet himself said that he was ten minutes late in occupying the hill), the Confederates would have had all night to position artillery as Hazlett did. If the Confederates had broken Vincent's brigade, they would have captured Hazlett's guns, ready and waiting on the crest, with full limbers of good-quality Northern ammunition. The Union left flank then would have been exposed and vulnerable no matter where Meade put it, since Little Round Top commanded the low ground to the north. Artillery could have weakened the line and enabled Confederate

infantry to roll up the flank. In addition, the Union center was certainly within range. On July 3, Hazlett's battery pounded the right flank of Pickett's Charge.

Did the fate of Gettysburg hang on Little Round Top?

Maybe, maybe not. Many factors combined for the Union victory. But Vincent's brigade, Hazlett's battery, and O'Rorke's 140th New York certainly helped save the Union army.

A Confederate Infantry Camp

After the thrill of enlistment wore off, new recruits learned that soldiering meant boredom in camp and endless drill. Pvt. Oliver Norton, of the 83rd Pennsylvania, wrote, "The first thing in the morning is drill, then drill, then drill again. Then drill, drill, a little more drill. Then drill, and lastly drill. Between drills, we drill and sometimes stop to eat a little and have a roll-call." But drilling was necessary for survival. A well-trained infantryman could load and fire his rifle two times a minute. A cannon crew could load and fire their piece twice a minute; if they fired point-blank, they could manage four shots a minute.

The soldiers typically used shelter or "dog" tents. Each soldier carried one half on the march, and when they stopped for the night, they would pair up their halves, matching buttons with buttonholes. Then they propped it up with sticks or rifles.

Confederate rations generally included cornbread or cornmeal, while the main staple of the Union soldiers' diet was hardtack

(crackers made from flour and water). No matter what rations were issued, a soldier always had to deal with worms in them. One Union soldier wrote about having to skim weevils off the surface of his coffee after soaking hardtack in it. But, he assured his readers, they "left no distinctive flavor."

Of all the rations issued, coffee was the most indispensable. Yankees had plenty, but Confederates had to make do with substitutes, such as ground up dried sweet potatoes or chicory. Soldiers quickly learned efficiency in preparing their coffee. After a day of marching, when the order came to halt, they would have fires built and water heating within five minutes. ★

Chapter 5

Pickett's Charge

ON JULY 3, GENERAL LEE SURMISED THAT GENERAL MEADE HAD probably weakened his center to reinforce his flanks the day before. If Lee used fresh troops, perhaps he could break through. He would mount a major assault, preceded by a massive artillery bombardment, on the Union center, where the troops had not dug entrenchments and were protected only by a low stone wall which formed an angle. The Confederates would use as a guiding mark a small clump or "copse" of trees that stood plainly visible on the ridge a mile away across the open fields.

But which troops should Lee use? He had only one fresh division—Maj. Gen. George Pickett's, of Longstreet's corps, which had arrived on the field that morning. To supplement them, Lee chose Heth's and Pender's divisions, which had fought on the first day but not on the second. Both Harry Heth and Dorsey Pender had been wounded, and now Gen. Johnston Pettigrew and Maj. Gen. Isaac Trimble commanded the respective divisions. Even though these troops were from Lt. Gen. A. P. Hill's corps, Lee placed Longstreet, his hard-hitting "old war horse," in overall command of the attacking forces.

Longstreet protested the idea of the charge, saying that "no fifteen thousand men ever arrayed for battle can take that position." Lee listened to him, but did not change his mind.

Lee did not know the horrible condition of Hill's two divisions. Because so many officers had

Lee's answer was to mount a major assault on the Union center.

fallen in the first day's fighting, Lee had not received reports on the casualties from that day. Now, after the troops took their positions along Seminary Ridge,

"The Fate of Gettysburg"

Scale: 1:72

Number of Cats:
US: 900   CS: 2,100

Dimensions:
7'9" x 5'9.5"

Date Created:
2000–2004

Lee rode along the lines to see that all was according to plan. What he saw shocked him. Not only were the ranks dreadfully thinned, but Lee could see bandaged wounds on some of the men who remained. "Many of these poor boys should go to the rear, they are not fit for duty," he said. Then, almost to himself, he added, "the attack must succeed." By now, it was too late to change the plan.

Col. E. P. Alexander, one of the Confederate army's finest artillery officers, would oversee Longstreet's First Corps artillery for the bombardment. His batteries had used much of their long-range ammunition the day before, and a prolonged duel would only waste what little they had. Alexander knew they must make every shot count and must cripple the Union forces "inside of an hour." Longstreet would rely on Alexander to gauge the effect of the bombardment and decide when to send the infantry forward.

MEANWHILE, IT WAS A QUIET, LAZY SORT OF A DAY ON Cemetery Ridge. Under the blazing sun, Union soldiers of the II Corps set up half-tents or blankets on sticks or bayonets to cast some shade. Along the line

Confederate artillery must cripple the Union forces in less than one hour.

where the stone wall petered out to nothing, some men worked on digging small breastworks.

Behind the crest, Brig. Gen. John Gibbon's staff cobbled together a fine lunch for Gibbon, commanding the division, and their corps commander, Maj. Gen. Winfield S. Hancock, as well as Meade and a couple of other generals with their

staffs. Army officers had to supply their own food, which generally proved difficult, but Gibbon's staff had quite a spread—a stewed rooster (which Gibbon considered "old and tough"), butter, potatoes, a cucumber pickle, and a loaf of bread that a hog had gotten hold of earlier. After lunch, the officers relaxed, chatting and enjoying coffee, tea, and cigars.

At 1:07 P.M., near the Peach Orchard, two guns fired. One shell landed among Lt. Alonzo Cushing's battery, near the Copse of Trees, overturning his officers' coffee and sending the men scurrying. The second shell exploded in the midst of the 19th Massachusetts, south of the Copse, tearing Lt. Sherman Robinson apart. At the signal, more than 120 Confederate cannons opened fire.

Nineteenth-Century Tech Woes

Technology is an amazing thing. Perhaps more amazing is the way we take it for granted. We gripe when it doesn't work, but how often do we think about the miracle of being able to click a mouse and have something "magically" happen on the screen?

In the 1860s, there were no radio signals and no WiFi. Communication depended on couriers (who could be shot) or the telegraph (whose wires could be cut). Before the war, however, Albert Myer and E. P. Alexander developed a nineteenth-century cell phone: a fully mobile communication system that did not require setting up a vulnerable landline (telegraph wires). Encryption was necessary, however—at the war's start, Alexander sided with the South and Myer with the North, which meant both armies had the technology and could read the messages.

What was this newfangled tech, you ask? The Signal Corps or "wig-wag" system. Designed for use over distances too great for a courier, the system consisted of stations set up miles apart on hills, mountains, or man-made towers. A typical station involved three men: one with a flag to send coded messages, one with a telescope to read incoming messages, and one to write it all down. They could even work at night, using torches instead of flags.

The message arrived as a series of numbers: a dip of the flag to the bearer's left was a 1, a dip to the right was a 2, and a dip to the front was a 3. Using prearranged codes, combinations of 1 and 2 represented letters or words, while 3 signaled the end of a word (3), sentence (33), or message (333).

The system worked quite well—except for the weakest part: the humans. Sending messages only worked if the receiving station noticed the continuous wig-wagging meant to get their attention.

Mid-morning on July 3, a signal station on Jack's Mountain, 10 miles from Gettysburg, noticed Garnett's and Kemper's brigades moving into position along Seminary Ridge. Frantically, the station signaled its relay on Little Round Top. The receiving station never noticed them, so their warning was never delivered.

Had the other station passed on the message, Union artillery could have pounded the waiting Confederate brigades. What would Lee have done if his last fresh division was mangled that morning?

Fortunately for the Union, the troops at the Angle managed to hold against Pickett's men, and the breakdown in communications technology did not result in the Union army's destruction. But there was probably a soldier on that mountain cussing out his technology!

Some things never change. ★

Gibbon bolted for the ridge, not even waiting for his groom to bring up his horse. As he topped the crest, a hellish panorama spread before him: the far ridge, lined with white smoke that obscured the trees and spread out of sight to left and right in one unbroken, menacing line. In the foreground, shells shrieked and moaned to explode among his men near the Copse. Solid shot bounded through the batteries and men, plowing up dirt and sending rocks and flesh flying. Every Confederate gun on the field seemed to focus its full fury on Gibbon's men.

The infantry hunkered behind their wall and tiny breastworks, flattening themselves into hollows in the ground or behind anything they could find. Moving like specters through the swirling smoke, Union artillerymen loaded their guns and sent their defiant reply to the Confederates, the iron 3-inch Ordnance rifles adding their deep-throated roars to the thunder around them, and the bronze Napoleons punctuating it with their characteristic "spang!"

Lt. Frank Haskell of Gibbon's staff joined the general, and together they walked toward the stone wall. As they passed Cushing's battery, two of Cushing's limbers exploded, sending fire, splinters, and shells high into the air. Unfazed, Gibbon

While nearly 300 cannons roared, the ground shook. Smoke turned the sky black.

Private Griffin

walked the entire length of his division's line, stopping now and then to stand with arms folded and observe the mayhem around him. One of his men recalled that his bearing "seem[ed] to say, Boys, this is the way to face danger. We all noticed it and many said, See There, see Gen. Gibbons [sic]." That day, he proved a staff officer right who had described him as "cool as a steel knife, always, and unmoved by anything and everything."

For the next hour, nearly three hundred cannons roared. The ground shook and heaved. Smoke hung over the fields, turning the sun red. Exploding shells turned the sky black. Legend says that in Washington, D.C., ladies heard the thunder and took in their laundry, and in Philadelphia, one hundred miles away, the ground trembled.

In the Angle, shell fragments wounded Lieutenant Cushing severely in the shoulder and groin, but he refused to leave his Battery A, 4th U.S. Artillery. At twenty-two years old, many considered him one of the best battery commanders in the army. As he limped among his guns, leaning on 1st Sgt. Frederick Fuger, he could see the dreadful pounding his men were taking.

Two limbers destroyed. Three of his six guns disabled. Men and horses torn apart by the shot and shells that struck and exploded around them every few seconds. An explosion mangled Private Griffin, a driver of one of the teams. In agony, he pulled out his revolver and shot himself in the head.

Brig. Gen. Henry Hunt commanded the Union artillery. He knew what such a barrage meant: infantry would advance after the guns fell silent. His batteries had to conserve their ammunition and wait. The batteries on Little Round Top and Cemetery Hill kept firing, but Hunt rode along Cemetery Ridge, ordering the batteries on the ridge to remain silent.

General Hancock of the II Corps was a large, commanding man—the type, Haskell believed, whom men would follow, even if he wore civilian clothes. But his power did not rest merely in being authoritative and commanding; his presence was reassuring. An officer noted, "One felt safe to be near him." He knew his men needed to see their commander firm and unshakable, so he mounted his black horse and rode along his lines. The horse acted up and the general switched to an aide's tall white-faced light bay. With his coat flapping open to show his signature spotless white shirt and accompanied by a single orderly carrying his II Corps flag, he rode along the ridge.

One of his brigade commanders, upon seeing him, pleaded, "General, the corps commander ought not to risk his life that way."

"There are times," Hancock replied, "when a corps commander's life does not count!" He continued on.

His men saw him and, in the words of a staff officer, "found courage longer to endure the pelting of the pitiless gale."

Hancock knew his presence alone was not enough to keep his men firm. The infantrymen would not understand the silent artillery. So, as he rode past the batteries, he

"There are times when a commander's life does not count!" replied Hancock.

ordered them to open fire. Faced with the looming Hancock rather than the absent Hunt, the II Corps battery commanders resumed firing.

Because of the high heat and humidity, smoke lingered near the ground. Cannons recoiled 10 feet when fired, so gunners needed to re-aim each time and relied on seeing where their shots fell in order to adjust for the next one. Unable to see through the smoke, the Confederate gunners began to fire high. Instead of striking the Angle, the shots fell behind the crest. Although Confederate fire mangled Lieutenant Cushing's and Lt. Fred Brown's batteries on either side of the Copse, the bombardment did not damage the Union center as much as Lee had hoped it would.

After more than an hour of bombardment, instead of the ten to fifteen minutes that Alexander had wanted, the Confederate artillery began running seriously low on ammunition. Finally, Alexander saw enemy guns pulling back and noticed the Union fire slacken. He sent a note to Pickett, "The 18 guns have been driven off. For God's sake, come quick, or we cannot support you. Ammunition nearly out." He had no way of knowing that Hunt had ordered the Union artillery to cease firing, he did not see Capt. Andrew Cowan's battery coming up to replace Brown's, and he could not tell that no other batteries had withdrawn.

Pickett, standing near Longstreet when the note arrived, asked, "General, shall I advance?"

Longstreet could not speak the order to advance; he could only bow his head.

Longstreet still could not bear to see his men cross those fields. But as a soldier, he had to obey Lee's orders. He bowed his head and nodded.

Pickett replied, "I shall lead my division forward, sir."

As the infantry formed ranks, Alexander went to fetch the nine howitzers he had set aside to move forward with them. The guns were gone! Now, Alexander had no artillery to send forward with the infantry and little long-range ammunition for his other guns to use in support. But it was too late to stop Pickett. The grand charge had begun.

A Very Hell of Fire

As the Confederate artillery began to overshoot on July 3, they hit General Meade's headquarters on Taneytown Road behind the Angle, as well as the field hospitals and artillery reserve. Meade and his staff rode to a safer place, but shells wrought havoc on the house and the horses tied in the yard.

Sam Wilkeson, a newspaper correspondent, recalled:

Every size and form of shell known . . . to American gunnery shrieked, whirled, moaned, whistled, and wrathfully fluttered over our ground. As many as six in a second, constantly

two in a second, bursting and screaming over and around the headquarters, made a very hell of fire. . . . They burst in the yard—burst next to the fence on both sides, garnished as usual with the hitched horses of aids [sic] and orderlies. The fastened animals reared and plunged with terror. Then one fell, then another. . . .

Through the midst of the storm of screaming and exploding shells, an ambulance, driven by its frenzied conductor at full speed, presented to all of us the marvelous spectacle of a horse going rapidly on three legs. A hinder one had been shot off at the hock.

The little house belonged to widow Lydia Leister, but she and her children had fled when the

armies arrived. After the battle, Lydia discovered that soldiers had destroyed her fences for firewood and trampled her entire crop of wheat—including the extra she had planted in order to finish paying off her land. All of her food except for a little flour had disappeared.

Both posts supporting her porch roof had been blown away. One shot had smashed a hole in her roof and knocked out a rafter.

Another had come through the end of her house and destroyed a bedstead. Rain on July 4 had undoubtedly soaked the upstairs through the holes in the roof.

The destruction did not end for Lydia when the army left the area. Sixteen horses lay rotting in her yard and spoiled her spring, so she had to dig a well. Her peach tree died when dead horses were burned near it. By the time a news correspondent visited two years

later, the only compensation Lydia had received for her losses was what she made from selling the bones of the horses. The correspondent found a woman "centered in her own losses" and caring nothing for the broader picture of what the country may have gained or lost by the battle. Can we blame her? ★

At 3:00 P.M., 12,000 Confederates stepped out of the trees along Seminary Ridge. The smoke had cleared, and now the sun shone brightly. Pettigrew's division formed the left of the attacking force. Behind them, Trimble's division came as support. Pickett's division formed the right: Brig. Gen. Richard Garnett led the left-hand brigade, Brig. Gen. James Kemper led the right-hand, and Brig. Gen. Lewis Armistead followed with the largest brigade as support.

A significant gap existed between Pettigrew and Garnett. Pickett's men would have

12,000 Confederates stepped out from the trees along Seminary Ridge.

to angle, or "oblique," to the left as they advanced, until they met up with Pettigrew. It was up to Garnett to make sure the two divisions met up correctly. If they did not, they

would strike the wall piecemeal, dividing their punch, and the attack would fail.

As the men formed ranks, Pickett galloped along his division's front and shouted, "Up, men, and to your posts! Don't forget today that you are from Old Virginia!"

General Armistead urged his men, "remember your wives, your mothers, your sisters and your sweethearts." He turned to Sgt. Leander Blackburn, carrying the flag of the 53rd Virginia, and said, "Sergeant, I want you and your men to plant your colors on those works. Do you think you can do it?"

"Yes, sir," Blackburn replied, "if God is willing."

On Cemetery Ridge, Lieutenant Cushing remained on his feet, despite the blood soaking his shell jacket and trousers. As the Confederate infantry emerged from the trees and formed on the distant ridge, Cushing ordered his men to roll his last two guns down to the wall, between the right flank of the 69th Pennsylvania and the left flank of the 71st Pennsylvania. So few men remained in the gun crews that the drivers of the caissons came to help work the guns.

withdrew, Brig. Gen. Alexander Webb knew his infantry brigade was in serious trouble. Nothing would prevent Confederates from pouring over the wall to his brigade's left. He sent a staff officer to find a battery to fill the gap. Cowan hesitated to disobey his existing orders, but agreed to bring up his guns when he saw Webb in the distance by the Copse of Trees, desperately waving his hat at him.

With the momentum of the cannon and limber behind them, the lead gun's team could not slow in time and passed the Copse before they managed to stop. With Confederate infantry beginning to advance, the gun crew had no time to move the 3-inch Ordnance rifle to

As Cushing's men tried to piece together their shattered battery, Capt. Andrew Cowan's 1st New York Independent Battery galloped up, its six guns and limbers jolting over the ground, the men seated on the limbers hanging on for dear life, the wheels rattling on the rocks, and the horses' harnesses jingling over the thunder of hooves. When Brown's battery

rejoin the rest of the battery. Cowan left the gun under the command of a sergeant while he commanded the five guns on the other side of the Copse.

General Lee watched the charge from a point of trees that jutted out from the tree line, near where the Virginia Memorial stands today. He sat on a large stump, holding in his left hand the reins of Traveller, his favorite iron gray horse. As the divisions advanced, he bowed his head in his right hand. One observer believed he was praying.

The Confederates stepped off with parade-ground precision. "The whole column is now within sight," Pvt. Randolph Shotwell of Garnett's

Capt. Cowan's separated cannon

8th Virginia recalled, "coming down the slope with steady step and superb alignment. The rustle of thousands of feet amid the stubble stirs a cloud of dust, like the dash of spray at the prow of a vessel."

Even Union soldiers stared in awe as the gray lines advanced: "I can see no end to the right nor left to the line that is coming." And then the Union artillery opened fire.

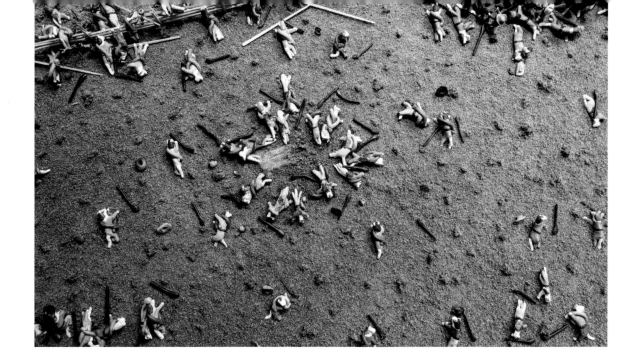

Batteries crammed onto Cemetery Hill fired at Col. John Brockenbrough's brigade on Pettigrew's left flank, pummeling a brigade that already had low morale. Pettigrew's main line avoided much fire, since the battery in their front had only short-range canister left and would have to wait for the Confederates to get closer. To Pickett's right, Hazlett's battery on Little Round Top, now under Lt. Benjamin Rittenhouse, had good visibility and elevation. They opened fire on Kemper's brigade, enfilading the line.

Rounds that overshot landed in Garnett's brigade. One solid shot alone hit twelve men in the 9th Virginia under Garnett. To Kemper's front, thirty-six guns under McGilvery opened

Union batteries fired on the Confederate lines, with full limbers at hand.

fire, with full limbers at hand, thanks to Hunt's foresight.

Nevertheless, Lt. John Lewis of Armistead's brigade recalled, "The crash of shell and solid shot, as they came howling and whistling through the lines, seemed to make no impression on the men. There was not a waver; but all was as steady as if on parade."

When Pettigrew's left had advanced about halfway across the fields, Union troops sprang into sight, charging straight at Brockenbrough's flank. The uncertain brigade did not wait to count Yankees. They had started out with only 600 men, and after getting pounded by Union artillery, they did not have the numbers—or at least the confidence—to face Yankees springing from the ground. The entire brigade headed for the rear.

The attackers were merely Union skirmishers with a lot of pluck. Lt. Col. Franklin Sawyer had been ordered to hold his position with his little 8th Ohio. Deciding not to sit idle and hope the Confederates would pass him by, he spread

his 160 men into one rank to make them look like more and charged. At the same time, about seventy-five men of the 125th New York also charged. After Brockenbrough's brigade disintegrated, the Union men settled themselves behind a fence and began firing at the rest of Pettigrew's flank.

As Garnett drew closer to the Emmitsburg Road, his left flank met up with Pettigrew's right. There was some jostling, but not much confusion. The timing was perfect. Now one solid front, the Confederates pressed on straight ahead. But even as the imposing line advanced, not

all was well. Kemper's brigade had finally passed out of sight of Rittenhouse's battery, but now Brig. Gen. George Stannard's Vermont brigade opened fire in their front. Kemper's men began drifting north, away from the Vermonters, crowding into Garnett's brigade—but even still the Confederate line pressed on, on to the crest.

Along both sides of the Emmitsburg Road, sturdy post-and-rail fences stood, designed to withstand cattle. As Garnett's brigade reached the road, about two-thirds of the way across the fields, Union infantry on Cemetery Ridge rose up from behind

the stone wall and poured a volley into the gray lines. Cushing's two guns and Cowan's battery opened with canister. In the face of this merciless fire, the Confederates had to cross the fences. Some rushed against the rails, trying to push the fences over with the force of the soldiers' massed weight. But the fences stood firm. The men had no choice but to wrestle the rails down one by one or crawl over or through the rails. Every second of delay meant more bullets and canister balls found targets.

On the left of Kemper's brigade, the 3rd Virginia passed through an orchard south of the

Codori house on the Emmitsburg Road. Col. Joseph Mayo noticed one of his captains looking "lazy and lackadaisical, and, if possible, more tired and bored than usual," with his sword resting on his shoulder as he told his company, "Don't crowd, boys; don't crowd."

Mayo commented on the Union fire around them, "Pretty hot, Captain."

The captain replied, "It's redicklous, Colonel; perfectly redicklous," which, Mayo noted, "in his vocabulary, meant as bad as bad could be."

In the center of Kemper's brigade, Col. Lewis B. Williams Jr. led his 1st Virginia from astride his little bay mare, Nelly. As they passed the Codori farm, Williams was struck in the shoulder. He fell from the saddle and landed on his sword, which killed him. Nelly continued with her regiment.

To the right of the 1st Virginia, Capt. John Smith of the 11th Virginia was struck in the right thigh as he pressed on from the Emmitsburg Road. Sergeant Kent took over command of Company G, but a bullet struck his leg as well, shattering a bone. Seeing him fall, Smith took command once again, ignoring his own wound.

As the Confederates drew closer to the Union line, the

Col. Lewis Williams on Nelly

skirmishers out in front met. Union skirmishers opened fire, and the Confederates fell back to be absorbed by the main force. Firing rippled along the line. Garnett rode behind his men, calling out, "Cease firing!" On the far right, Mayo saw a tall light bay horse galloping along the Union skirmish line. Admiring the officer's courage, he shouted, "Don't shoot him! Don't shoot him!" His men obeyed, and General

Hancock survived to continue strengthening his corps.

Behind the stone wall, Lieutenant Cushing leaned on Sergeant Fuger, weak and relaying his orders through the sergeant. As his guns switched to double canister, he moved to help out at gun #4. When loading a cannon, one man would cover the vent hole in the breech with his thumb while the charge was rammed home. Otherwise, escaping gases

For Honor

Confederate officers were ordered not to ride their horses in the charge, since it would make them easier targets. Despite that, quite a few rode. Of them all, General Garnett perhaps had the best excuse to ride—or to avoid the charge altogether. During the march up from Virginia, a horse had kicked Garnett and seriously injured his leg, forcing him to ride the rest of the way in an ambulance. Now, on July 3, barely able to walk, he could have stayed behind. But nothing would prevent him from leading his men forward. Why?

The year before, Gen. Thomas "Stonewall" Jackson had accused Garnett of cowardice, after the latter pulled his men out of an untenable position. Although his friends knew Garnett was no coward, the

Gen. Richard B. Garnett

accusation haunted him. Even now, months after Jackson's death, Garnett felt he had to prove his courage. He could not sit out Pickett's Charge.

Garnett rode his big dark-bay Thoroughbred named Red Eye, waving his black hat and urging his men, "Faster, men! Faster, but don't double-quick.

Save your wind and ammunition for the final charge." The last his men saw of him, he was nearing the stone wall. Some say he fell riddled with bullets. Others say he fell in front of Cushing's guns. Many saw Red Eye galloping to the rear, his saddle covered with blood. After the charge, one of Garnett's men saw the general's friend Capt. Charles Linthicum weeping with his head resting on Red Eye's neck.

No one knows what happened to Garnett's body; it is assumed he lies in an unknown grave with his men. But no one can doubt his courage, shown by his calm, solid leadership across the open fields, through the storm of canister and bullets, all the way to the stone wall. ★

Left: Col. Dennis O'Kane
Above: Lt. Alonzo Cushing

would fan any sparks inside, which could then ignite the powder being rammed down the barrel. A leather "thumbstall" protected the man's thumb. Cushing found the thumbstall charred and useless, a testament to his men's desperate work ever since the bombardment began hours earlier.

He covered the vent with his bare thumb. The shot was rammed down, forcing the hot gases before it. Cushing gritted his teeth and left his thumb in place as long as was necessary. By the time he stepped away from the gun, his thumb was burned to the bone.

In the 1st Virginia, the entire color guard fell, one after the other, carrying the flag. Private Lawson then picked up the flag and was struck in the right arm. Private Polak took it from him and reached the wall before he, too, was wounded. Their commanders fared no better. Colonel Williams, killed; Major Langley, wounded; Captain Norton, wounded; Captain Davis, wounded. After Davis, the regiment had no apparent commander—but the men kept on.

Kneeling behind the stone wall by the Copse of Trees, the 69th Pennsylvania waited under the watchful eye of their colonel. Just as officers in the

Revolution had urged their men decades earlier, Col. Dennis O'Kane ordered his men to hold their fire until they saw the whites of the Confederates' eyes. Now, as Garnett's brigade neared, the Irishmen rose.

As they did, to their right, Cushing fell, killed by a bullet through the mouth. Fuger turned to catch him with his right arm, and Cushing's blood splattered over the sergeant's uniform. Fuger lowered him to the ground with his head to the enemy.

Command passed to Lieutenant Milne, but he fell, mortally wounded in the abdomen.

The remnants of Battery A now belonged to Sergeant Fuger.

With the Confederates a couple hundred yards away, Fuger ordered treble canister. It was a desperate gamble, seeking to do three times the damage to the relentless gray lines, but risking explosion of the gun. But with Garnett pressing close, Fuger's men needed every shot to buy time to reload the guns, and only treble canister could accomplish that.

Hancock's entire line was now engulfed in fire and smoke. On the left, the 7th Michigan

Treble canister was risky, but a dangerous gamble the artillerymen had to take.

and 20th Massachusetts fired into Kemper's brigade, causing them to crowd into Garnett even more. In the center, at the

Angle, the situation looked grim for Gibbon's division. Approximately 3,000 Confederates of Pickett's division and Archer's brigade faced 375 Union infantry and eight guns low on canister. On the right, things looked slightly better for Brig. Gen. Alexander Hays's division of 1,700 men. Together with eleven guns, they faced 2,500 under Pettigrew. General Hays waited until Pettigrew's men were tangled in a fence before ordering his men to stand and fire.

As Garnett's and Kemper's brigades neared the stone wall,

Old and New

The soldiers on both sides of Pickett's Charge were a microcosm of America, with "old family" sons and new immigrants mingled together.

Some Irishmen in the 69th Pennsylvania had arrived in the United States only a few months before they enlisted. Among the men of Alexander Hays's division stood Joseph Pierce, a Chinese man, complete with the stereotypical long pigtail.

At the other end of the spectrum, General Armistead's uncle, Maj. George Armistead, had defended Fort McHenry against the British in the War of 1812. His defense inspired Francis Scott Key to pen "The Star-Spangled Banner." In Armistead's brigade, Pvt. Robert Tyler Jones was the grandson of President John Tyler, and Col. William Aylett was the grandson of the great patriot Patrick Henry.

The colonel of the 20th Massachusetts, Paul Revere, was a descendent of *the* Paul Revere of the American Revolution. Colonel Revere fell mortally wounded in the bombardment before Pickett's Charge. Gen. Alexander Webb's grandfather, Samuel B. Webb, was a minuteman at Lexington in 1775, where the American Revolution began with "the shot heard round the world." ★

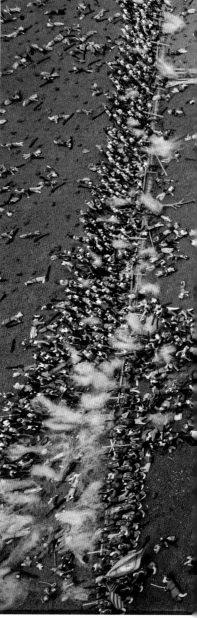

Armistead's brigade approached the Emmitsburg Road, their general tramping ahead of them. As they started up the final slope, Kemper appeared through the smoke, riding for Armistead. "General, hurry up," Kemper called to him, "My men can stand no more." As Kemper wheeled his horse and rode off, Armistead turned to his men and ordered the double-quick.

Behind Armistead, in the 53rd Virginia, Sergeant Blackburn fell mortally wounded by a shell fragment. Corporal Scott took up the flag, ran fifteen feet, and was killed. Cpl. Robert Tyler Jones took up the colors and was immediately wounded in the arm. Nevertheless, he kept the flag and continued on.

In an effort to stop his men drifting north, Kemper waved his sword and shouted, "There are the guns, boys, go for them!" But he pointed northward,

making the confusion worse. Then a bullet struck him and he reeled in the saddle. His orderly caught him and lowered him to the ground. Colonel Mayo of the 3rd Virginia, now in command of the brigade, tried to stem the drifting tide with help from a couple of other officers.

He recalled later, "Everything was a wild kaleidoscopic whirl."

In Garnett's right-hand regiments, it was every man for himself, with some men going forward and some facing right. Rifles crossed as some fired at the Yankees behind the stone wall and others fired at

Stannard's men. In the 18th Virginia, Pvt. James Clay glimpsed Garnett, astride Red Eye, approaching the wall. Then a shell fragment struck Clay in the head. Blinded by blood streaming into his eyes, he stumbled into some large rocks. Nearby, Capt. Edmund Cocke caught a

glimpse of his brother William, a lieutenant. A bullet grazed Edmund on the head, knocking him down. In the short time it took him to struggle to his feet, his brother disappeared. He never saw William again.

Garnett's men dashed forward, rushing the wall. Lieutenant Finley of the 56th Virginia passed so close to Cushing's cannons that he felt the heat of the guns' blasts. The 28th Virginia followed their colors carried by Colonel Allen. He fell, mortally wounded, and handed the flag to Lieutenant

Confederates swarmed over the wall as Union color bearers planted their flags.

Lee. The 71st Pennsylvania gave way before the 28th Virginia. Lieutenant Lee leaped onto the wall—the first of Garnett's

brigade—and stood waving the flag. A bullet struck the staff, splintering it. Colonel Allen, lying on his back, asked a nearby man about the flag. Then, content that his men had taken the wall, he put his hat on his head and died. Along the wall, color bearers planted their regimental colors on the rocks as Garnett's men swarmed over.

Lt. Haskell, watching the 71st Pennsylvania fall back and Confederates pour over the wall, thought that "the fate of Gettysburg hung upon a spider's single thread." He

A Father's Love

As Pickett's men started across the fields, Capt. Michael Spessard of the 28th Virginia probably felt more anxiety than usual. In the battle line with him marched his only son, Hezekiah. The young man had just joined his father that January. Now, as the line advanced, Spessard's worst nightmare came true. Hezekiah fell, mortally wounded. Michael Spessard could not stop—as the captain, he must continue to lead his men. But he paused, gave the boy his canteen and kissed him, and then picked up his sword and continued on.

But a father cannot forget his son, even when duty calls, and every thought, as he marched onward, step after step, was filled with the sight of his son, lying on the bloody ground behind him. By the time Spessard reached the stone wall, he was furious. Leaping over the wall, he fought the Union soldiers with his sword. Three soldiers managed to wrestle the sword away from him, but when they

Capt. Michael Spessard

demanded his surrender, he picked up rocks and pelted the men, chasing them away.

When the charge failed, Spessard retreated with his regiment, found his son, and saw that Hezekiah was treated at a field hospital. Despite the care, Hezekiah died on July 19.

Captain Spessard received a promotion for his gallantry at the stone wall. But surely he would rather have forgone the promotion—if it meant he could still have his son alive with him. ★

My Brave Horse, Dick

For many soldiers, a horse was not only a mode of transportation, but a close friend. In his account of Pickett's Charge, Lieutenant Haskell wrote about "Dick," whom he described as "my brave horse." Despite a serious wound to his right thigh and three bullets in his body, Dick carried Haskell back and forth at the gallop as the lieutenant urged men forward and summoned reinforcements.

Lt. Frank Haskell on Dick

Not until their duty was over did Dick lie down and finally succumb to his mortal wounds. "Good conduct in men under such circumstances," Haskell wrote, "might result from a sense of duty—his was the result of his bravery." Haskell finished by expressing his wish that, if there be a heaven for horses, "in those shadowy clover fields [Dick] may nibble blossoms forever." ★

galloped to the left, to find help from Hall's brigade—the same Norman Hall who had saved the flag at Fort Sumter.

Kemper's brigade struck the wall next, but Stannard still caused trouble on its right. By now, perhaps a quarter of the brigade had bent back to face the Vermonters, and the remainder still crowded left into Garnett, crossing diagonally in front of the Union lines.

Colonel Mayo of the 3rd Virginia held his ground near the stone wall with a small band of rallied men. Picking up a rifle, Mayo joined his men in firing at the Yankees. A sudden hiss, "like the hooded cobra's whisper of death," and a shell's explosion knocked him down, momentarily blacking him out. Picking himself up, he remained in command.

The 1st Virginia still lost officers. Captain Hallinan, killed; Lieutenant Dooley, shot through both thighs; Lieutenant Caho, wounded in the thigh. But the regiment continued to inch forward. Nelly the mare still advanced with her men.

The 20th Massachusetts of Hall's brigade fired volley after volley until the Confederates to their front broke. Suddenly with nothing to do, they looked to their right and saw Confederates pouring over the wall by the Copse. Just then, Haskell galloped up, looking for reinforcements.

But when the order came to move, the men could not hear their officers over the chaos around them. The regiment became thoroughly confused, so the officers ran out in front and pointed their swords to the trees. The men got the hint and ran pell-mell for the Copse.

Captain Smith still limped along with his company of the 11th Virginia. He remembered later that his men struck the Union line at "a hasty trench

72nd Pennsylvania

and embankment," where the stone wall had petered out. In front of the Union position lay an area of rough ground with enough vegetation to afford some cover. Most of the regiment stayed there and fired at Cowan's artillerymen.

General Gibbon rode to his division's left to start a flanking movement, but before he could, a bullet passed through his left shoulder and shattered his shoulder blade. Blood streamed down his arm and dripped from his hand. Weak from loss of blood, he relinquished command of his division to Brig. Gen. William Harrow.

General Hancock also saw the opportunity to flank the Confederates. If Stannard moved his Vermonters northward, he could crumble the gray lines. Turning his tall bay's head, Hancock spurred the horse down the crest.

In the Angle, the 72nd Pennsylvania had come up from reserve and halted on the crest just before the Confederates rushed the wall. Now, they stood immovable, firing and holding off the Confederate surge. In a stalemate, the two sides slugged away at each other.

General Garnett and Red Eye

Riding behind his men, General Garnett fell dead. Private Clay, blinded by blood, still lay among the rocks, now joined by Capt. Archer Campbell, whose arm had been broken by a ball. All of a sudden, a shadow flew over them—Garnett's horse, Red Eye, leaping over the rocks, galloping to the rear, stirrups flapping, the empty saddle covered with blood, his own blood streaming from a ragged hole in his right shoulder.

To the left of Garnett's brigade, Col. Birkett D. Fry led Gen. James Archer's brigade in Pettigrew's division. The brigade had been mangled and their general captured on the first day, but they still had fight left in them. Blood soaked Fry's uniform from a shoulder wound sustained during the bombardment and a thigh wound during the advance. Finally weakening from his wounds, he planted a flag at the Angle and remained there, urging his men, "Go on; it will not last five minutes longer!" But the Confederate surge stalled and ebbed back. The brigades were a jumbled mess by now, jammed 15 to 30 feet deep at the wall, regiments of Archer, Garnett, and Kemper all mingled together.

Col. Birkett D. Fry

The stalled Confederates needed someone to lead them forward one more time.

On the crest, General Webb and Lieutenant Haskell urged the 72nd Pennsylvania forward. But the regiment did not move. Webb tried to lead them forward with their own flag, but the color bearer, Sgt. William Finecy, refused to let it go. After wrestling over the staff for a few moments, Webb gave up.

And now Armistead's brigade came up. Pvt. William Monte of the 9th Virginia glanced at his watch and commented, "We have been just nineteen minutes coming," and then a shell killed him. Armistead's right-hand regiments joined Kemper's men in the rough ground and in the fight with the Vermonters.

The 14th Virginia pressed up to the 69th Pennsylvania.

Col. James Hodges fell dead only four feet from the wall, buried in a pile of dead and wounded, including three or four other officers. The brigade stalled, mixed in with Garnett's and Kemper's men. The Confederates needed someone to lead them forward one more time.

Placing his black slouch hat on the tip of his sword and raising it so the men could see it, General Armistead pushed through the mass. He crossed diagonally in front of the 69th Pennsylvania to reach the wall that Garnett's men held and urged his men forward. The Confederates rushed the wall once more. Cushing's #4 gun fired their last round of canister at Confederates only a few feet away from the wall.

Out of ammunition, the artillerymen fought the swarming Confederates with pistols, handspikes, rammers, and even their fists until Fuger ordered them to withdraw. Some obeyed, and some joined the 69th Pennsylvania to continue fighting.

Lieutenant Cushing's artillerymen join the 69th Pennsylvania

"They have broken through; the colors are coming . . . let me go in there!"

Gen. Alexander Webb

Shouting, "Give them the cold steel, boys! Who will follow me?" Armistead crossed the wall near gun #4, laying his left hand on the left wheel to steady himself as he climbed over the rocks. Then he trotted forward, heading for Cushing's rear guns.

Farther down the ridge, the 19th Massachusetts and 42nd New York saw the break-through and knew Webb's men needed reinforcements, but no one had brought orders for Hall's brigade to move. Now, seeing their corps commander riding past, Col.

Arthur Devereaux of the 19th Massachusetts jumped to stop him. "See, general," he called up to the towering Hancock. "They have broken through; the colors are coming over the stone wall; let me go in there!"

Hancock, his blood fired up, shot back, "Go in there pretty God-damned quick!" It was all the regiments needed. The men cheered and rushed for the trees.

With the 72nd Pennsylvania still refusing to charge, Webb headed for the 69th Pennsylvania who doggedly held their

ground at the stone wall. As he crossed the distance between the regiments, Webb saw Armistead cross the wall and pass him. A bullet grazed Webb's thigh, but he kept going.

As Confederates poured over the wall after Armistead, the 69th Pennsylvania bent its right wing back at a right angle. "We followed and fired and loaded as we fell back," one man wrote, "looking and praying for help." Companies A and I formed a line that ran from the wall

The 69th fought hand-to-hand with rocks, fists, and clubbed muskets.

Cpl. Robert Tyler Jones

What Would You Do?

The 69th Pennsylvania must have felt alone at the stone wall. On their left, some of Cowan's canister struck them in the back or kicked up rock splinters. On the right, Confederates turned the 69th's flank and threatened their rear. Still, the Union soldiers kept up a terrific fire and refused to budge.

Why did they stay? Was it because their duty told them to? Was it because their friends in the regiment stayed? Perhaps they felt a need to prove themselves. These men were Irish immigrants. In the 1800s, immigrants—especially the Irish—were looked down upon and feared. Even

General Webb despised them. Ironically, he now fought alongside them, his only regiment remaining at the wall.

Perhaps they fought with such tenacity because the war had come to Pennsylvania, their

new homeland. Hailing from Philadelphia, these men fought personally to drive the invaders from their doorstep. Whatever their reasons, the Irishmen of the 69th stood firm beneath the flags of their past and their future—the green of Ireland and the Union Stars and Stripes.

If you were a soldier in the 69th Pennsylvania, what would you do? Would you endure enemy and friendly fire for a country that did not accept you? Would you stay, out of a sense of duty or peer pressure? Would you retreat, rather than face capture when the enemy surrounded your lone regiment? What would you do? ★

---

into the Copse itself until the underbrush stopped them.

Company F's captain was killed before he could relay the order, so the company was overwhelmed before they learned of the move. Company D, on the point of the right angle in the line, fought hand-to-hand with rocks, fists, and clubbed muskets.

Along the wall, Kemper's men pressed in close against the main line of the 69th

Pennsylvania, and the Union regiment's colors moved back half a dozen feet. "Everybody was loading and firing as fast as they could," one Pennsylvanian recalled. "We thought we were all gone." And still they held.

Cpl. Robert Tyler Jones, still carrying the colors of the 53rd Virginia despite his wounded arm, leaped onto the stone wall. He waved the flag and fell, severely wounded. Lt. Hutchings Carter picked up

the flag and carried it forward. Jones remained leaning against the wall, still full of fight and wielding his pistol. Carter followed Armistead, along with a couple hundred Confederates.

Col. John Bowie Magruder of the 57th Virginia climbed over the wall to Armistead's left. Seeing Cushing's guns, he shouted, "They are ours!" Then a bullet from the 72nd Pennsylvania struck him from the front and another from the 69th Pennsylvania passed through his arm from the right. The bullets crossed in his chest, and the 23-year-old colonel fell mortally wounded.

Lieutenant Colonel Carrington of the 18th Virginia reached the wall with his regiment's colors and also fell wounded. Colors of the 57th, 53rd, and 14th Virginia were planted near Cushing's rear guns.

As Armistead reached the rear guns, he turned and laid his left hand on one of them, calling out, "Turn the guns!" Then a bullet struck him in the left arm and another hit him in the right leg, below the knee. Dropping his sword, he winced and bent over, his left hand against his stomach. He staggered a couple steps, and fell. He lay there, grasping his left arm with his right hand. Near him, Lt. Col. Rawley Martin also fell, his right thigh shattered near the hip and his left leg and foot bloody from three lesser wounds. His friend, Sgt. Thomas Tredway, rushed to help him and fell mortally wounded across the lieutenant colonel. Bullets struck Lt. Thomas Holland of the 28th Virginia in the face and neck, and he collapsed near Armistead, semiconscious.

When Armistead fell, some Confederates returned to the

Col. John Bowie Magruder

Gen. Lewis Armistead

shelter of the stone wall. Others sought cover around Cushing's guns and fired at the 72nd Pennsylvania, which remained silhouetted against the sky. Some worked their way into the Copse of Trees, threatening the rear of the 69th Pennsylvania, with nothing to slow them but the underbrush.

Hancock found Stannard already moving his Vermonters northward, having had the same thought as Hancock. Stannard's men on the Confederate right and the 8th Ohio on the left now had the massive attacking column compressed to a mere 400 yards in width. And yet the contest was still far from decided.

As Hancock turned to head back up his lines, a bullet passed through his saddle and struck him in the right

Union troops pressed in on both flanks, but Confederates fought on.

thigh. Officers lowered him to the ground, and Stannard quickly tied his handkerchief around Hancock's leg. Pushing his revolver's barrel between the handkerchief and leg, he twisted the gun to tighten the bandage into a makeshift tourniquet. Still concerned for his corps and now out of danger of bleeding to death, Hancock refused to be moved until the fighting was decided. Not long after, Stannard, too, was wounded in the leg.

Urged up by Lieutenant Haskell and General Hancock, the 20th Massachusetts and

42nd New York piled into the Copse, with the 19th Massachusetts close behind.

Maj. Edmund Rice of the 19th found the Copse "fairly jammed" with Confederates. The 1st Minnesota also rushed to join the mass of Union troops. Corporal Dehn, carrying the colors, was wounded in the hand, and Cpl. Henry O'Brien picked up the flag.

Crammed together, at least six men deep, Union soldiers fired over and around each other, and their bullets sometimes hit their fellow soldiers from behind. Some men lobbed rocks at the

Half a dozen Union regiments poured into the Copse.

Confederates over the heads in front. Neither side gave way.

Men on both sides looked over their shoulders for support. The 72nd Pennsylvania still stood on the crest, facing over a thousand soldiers of Pickett's shattered brigades behind the stone wall. The 69th

Decimated But Not Done

The 1st Minnesota Regiment had been decimated on July 2, when Hancock threw them against an entire brigade to buy time to bring up more troops. Most sources say only Company C, serving as division Provost Guard, came into the Copse on July 3. But earlier that day during lunch, Meade, expecting an attack on his center, commented that it would be best to have the men of the Provost Guard in the ranks today. Gibbon agreed and sent Company C to rejoin the regiment. The group that entered the Copse included the regimental colors, carried by Corporal Dehn, the last of the color guard, indicating the presence of the entire regiment, so reduced as to look like a company. ★

Pennsylvania still held their ground, their left flank trusting Cowan's five guns to hold Kemper's men back. "Whichever side could get a motion forward," Colonel Devereux believed, "must surely win."

Major Rice of the 19th Massachusetts wrote, "This was one of those periods in action which are measureable by seconds. The men near seemed to fire very slowly. Those in the rear, though coming up at a run, seemed to drag their feet."

In the rough ground, Captain Smith of the 11th Virginia looked back across the fields and "could see nothing but dead and wounded men and horses . . . my heart never in my life sank as it did then."

Again, Haskell urged the 72nd Pennsylvania to advance, and finally someone responded.

Sergeant Murphy ran forward with the flag. One man followed him. Halfway to the wall, both fell. At the sight of the flag striking the ground, the regiment gave a tremendous yell and charged.

In the Copse, Corporal O'Brien, still gripping the shattered staff of the 1st Minnesota's colors, ran forward. His regiment sprang after him. Suddenly, all of the Union soldiers in the Copse gave a yell and charged, their flags to the front.

As Major Rice motioned to the 19th Massachusetts, a bullet tore his sword from his hand, another struck his cap's visor, stunning him and whirling him around, and a third struck him in the abdomen. As he fell, his men rushed past

Sergeant Murphy

him. Corporal O'Brien fell with two wounds as the two sides clashed in a final hand-to-hand melee. Corporal Irvine took up the flag and kept going.

The counterattack broke the Confederates. Some retreated across the wall; many just

Cpl. Henry O'Brien

Col. Arthur Devereaux (left) and Maj. Edmund Rice

surrendered. Union soldiers captured flag after flag. In the Angle alone, the colors of Garnett's 18th, 19th, 28th, and 56th Virginia; of Armistead's 9th, 14th, 53rd, and 57th Virginia; and of Kemper's 3rd Virginia fell into Union hands. Lieutenant Carter, carrying the 53rd's colors, surrendered and left his regiment's flag at one of Cushing's guns. Union soldiers found the 28th Virginia's flag leaning up against one of the guns as well.

In the rough ground, Captain Smith ordered the remnant of his 11th Virginia to fall back, but he stayed behind to bind up his leg wound with a towel. Capt. Robert Douthat stayed with him and began firing at the approaching Vermonters. Smith, thinking the calm movements of his fellow captain meant the enemy was still reasonably far away, took the time to properly bind his wound. Finished, Smith looked up and was shocked to see the Yankees only 75 yards away. "Douthat, what are you doing?" he exclaimed.

Douthat tossed aside his rifle. "It's time to get away from here," he replied. The two men ran.

In the 1st Virginia, Lieutenant Reeve had taken command as the regiment approached the wall. Now, wounded and with less than a dozen men left, he and the remnants headed for the rear. Their colors remained near the wall and were captured along with those of the 7th Virginia. The regiment suffered 62 percent casualties. Only two officers were not killed or wounded.

The 26th North Carolina lost 630 men of 900 during the 3-day battle.

The mare Nelly made it back to Seminary Ridge, limping and crippled. An artilleryman caught her, and eventually she found her way back to Colonel Williams's servant, Harry. Colonel Mayo recalled how Harry "asked me what I thought old master would say when she was all belonging to Mars Lewis he had to take home."

To Pickett's left, Pettigrew's and Trimble's men had no more luck against General Hays's brigade. Some Confederates managed to cross the wall, but without support they, too, were forced back. The 26th North Carolina, under Pettigrew, had begun the campaign with

26th North Carolina

around 900 men. In the first day's fighting, they lost over 500. Now, they lost another 130. In the 11th North Carolina, only 80 men remained of 650.

On Seminary Ridge, General Lee rode out to meet the remnants of his divisions. "It's all my fault," he said. "I thought my men were invincible."

General Pickett had watched from the Codori farm area, where, as division commander, he could oversee the charge and be found easily

General Pickett lost two-thirds of his men in the charge. He never forgave General Lee.

by couriers. As he returned to Seminary Ridge, he met Lee, who told him he must see to his division. He replied, "General Lee, I have no division now." He never forgave Lee.

Pickett was not far wrong in his evaluation. Roll calls taken by each unit in the following days showed the staggering consequences of the charge. Of approximately 12,000 men who advanced, nearly 6,500 were killed, wounded, or captured. Pickett's division lost 67 percent

of its men, Pettigrew's 60 percent, and Trimble's 52 percent. In Garnett's brigade alone, out of 1,287 men, only about 300 made it back to Seminary Ridge, according to the report of Maj. Charles Peyton of the 19th Virginia, now commanding the brigade. Company D of the 56th Virginia lost every man killed or wounded. In Kemper's 3rd Virginia, Company F lost all but one man.

On an emotional level, at a time when the flag of a regiment was its heart and soul, thirteen of the fifteen regiments of Pickett's division lost their colors to Union captors. Only the colors of Kemper's 11th and 24th Virginia made it back to Seminary Ridge.

The Battle of Gettysburg was over. General Meade had passed the supreme test; he would retain command of the Army

of the Potomac throughout the rest of the war. General Lee had failed to win a great victory on Northern soil, and his army had suffered devastating losses, particularly in officers. The Army of Northern Virginia would never be the same. Lt. John James of the 11th Virginia said it best when he wrote of Pickett's Charge: "We gained nothing but glory and lost our bravest men."

"A Spirit in My Feet Said 'Go' and I Went"

Photography was still new in 1861; only thirty-five years had elapsed since the world's first photograph was taken. In the United States, Mathew Brady was well known for his photographs of famous people, including Daniel Webster and President Zachary Taylor. When the war began, Brady decided he had to document it through photography. In answer to friends who worried about his leaving a successful career to risk the dangers of war, he replied, "A spirit in my feet said 'Go' and I went." He was not alone; many independent and government-employed photographers followed the armies on both sides.

Brady used the "wet-plate" collodion process, which required two men. One man focused the camera while the other poured a mixture of chemicals, called "collodion," on a glass plate. After letting the collodion set, he dipped the plate—in darkness—in a silver nitrate solution to make it light-sensitive, then placed the plate in a holder which he would slide into the camera. The photographer only had about ten minutes after pouring the collodion to take and develop the photograph before the chemicals would dry.

Developing the photograph required a careful, multistep process to preserve or "fix" the image. The result was a negative from which multiple prints

(continued)

could be made. Alternatively, the negative could be backed with black fabric or paper (an *ambrotype*) or a black metal plate (a *tintype*).

The wet-plate process only needed seconds of exposure to take a photograph outdoors, but that was still too long to allow pictures of battles. Even so, several action photographs were attempted. Alexander Gardner's photo taken at the battle of Antietam on September 17, 1862, shows smoke drifting over waiting reinforcements. On September 8, 1863, a Confederate at Fort Sumter photographed three Union monitors as they bombarded Fort Moultrie—one

can even see the smoke from the turrets as they fire!

The work that photographers accomplished as they traveled with the armies was

Various styles of a "What-is-it"

nothing short of amazing, since they had to transport their chemicals and fragile glass plates over rough roads and terrain. They often had a large wagon to carry the equipment and a smaller dark-room buggy—dubbed a "What-is-it" by Union soldiers—which could be used alone when the photographer needed to travel light.

Brady's photographs showed his viewers a war unlike anything they knew. Civilians were used to seeing lithographs and sketches of neat battle lines rushing forward or

"Soldiers" AUTHORS' COLLECTION

an officer's tragic but glorious death. Photographs showed friends or sons, ready to fight for the glorious cause and starry flag, or dashing generals with their gold braid and jaunty hats. What a shock these people received when they entered Brady's exhibit "The Dead at Antietam" and saw, for the first time, the grisly reality of war.

Oliver Wendell Holmes, father of the U.S. Supreme Court justice of that name, wrote of the exhibit, "Let him who wishes to know what the war is look at this series of illustrations. These wrecks of manhood thrown together in careless heaps . . . were but alive yesterday." Another viewer wrote, "If he has not brought bodies and laid them in our dooryards and along our streets, he has done something very like it."

The Civil War was a time for experimentation with photographic techniques and subject matter. It was a time to record the images of great men, notable women, and the ravages of war that otherwise would not have reached the citizens in the farther reaches of the country . . . or of time.

Through this remarkable medium, we can gaze into the past. We see Richmond, destroyed. We see Maj. Gen. William Tecumseh Sherman's grit and determination. We see the tenderness of a mother with her baby—the style of clothing is different, but some things never change.

We see the faces of the dead—nameless, awaiting burial . . . or as their families would remember them, gazing steadily into the camera in a new uniform, with sword or revolver in hand, ready to take on the enemy and looking forward to returning home again. We see the ones they left behind: wives, children, sweethearts.

We can even see stories we read about, brought through time exactly as they appeared 150 years ago. In photographs of Fort Sumter, the cannons fired by Private Carmody still sit recoiled, and the Columbiad fired from its recoiled position still lies fallen, halfway into the stair tower, next to the howitzer it dismounted.

Take some time to study a photograph from the past. What can you see? ★

Chapter 6

The Assault on Battery Wagner

MANY ISSUES BOILED OVER INTO THE CIVIL WAR, including the abolition of slavery. Even Northerners, however, considered the war a "white man's war" and did not permit black men to join the army. Many thought black soldiers would run away as soon as they saw a Confederate. One governor said it was "a *white man's* government," and that "white men are able to defend it." As a result, the Northern army used blacks only for manual labor. That began to change on January 1, 1863, when the Emancipation Proclamation decreed that black men would be "received into the armed service of the United States."

Early in February 1863, Governor John Andrew of Massachusetts issued the Civil War's first call for "colored" soldiers. The 54th Massachusetts Volunteer Infantry was formed. Many recruits came from outside Massachusetts, even from as far away as Canada, the Caribbean, and various southern states. Charles and Lewis Douglass, sons of the great Frederick Douglass, also enlisted.

The governor asked Capt. Robert Gould Shaw to command the 54th Massachusetts as its colonel. At first, Captain Shaw refused. He was in a good position in his current regiment and had lost friends with that unit. He did not know what his beloved fiancée would think of

the proposal. He also knew that command of a black regiment would subject him to ridicule. At the same time, he felt ashamed. Raised in an antislavery family,

The Emancipation Proclamation made the 54th Massachusetts possible.

he could not help but wonder what they thought of his refusal. He worried that his mother, an ardent abolitionist, would "think I am shirking my duty."

"I Want You to Prove Yourselves"

Scale: 1:48 **Number of Cats:** US: 131; CS: 41

Dimensions: 1'8" x 2'0.5"

Date Created: Oct. 1999–Jan. 21, 2000

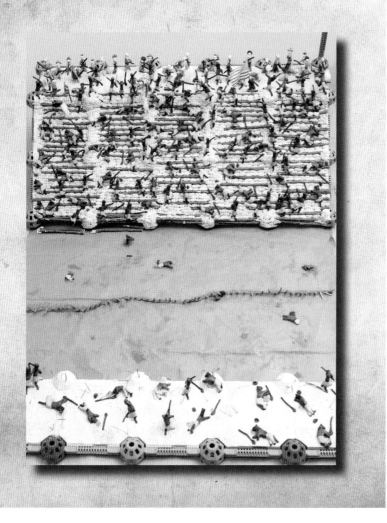

FOR SOME TIME, COLONEL SHAW WAS UNABLE TO GET ORDERS TO take his regiment into battle. Their first combat finally came on July 16, 1863, in a skirmish on James Island, South Carolina. To the regiment's left stood the 10th Connecticut, a white regiment. This unit had a river on their left and a swamp to the rear. If the 54th Massachusetts broke and ran, the Connecticut regiment would be surrounded. The Confederates attacked, but the 54th Massachusetts contested every inch as they retreated in an orderly fashion. They held long enough for the 10th Connecticut to pull out of their dangerous position.

One Connecticut soldier wrote home, "But for the bravery of three companies of the Massachusetts Fifty-fourth (colored), our whole regiment would have been captured . . . They fought like heroes." Later, as the 54th Massachusetts marched past the camps of other white regiments, the soldiers greeted them with the cries: "Well done! we heard your guns!" and "Hurrah, boys! you saved the Tenth Connecticut!"

Two days later, the regiment faced their greatest test.

After two days of further consideration, Shaw changed his mind and accepted the commission. He wrote his father, "Tell Mother I have not wavered at all, since my final decision. I feel that if we can get the men, all will go right."

Still Unequal

The Emancipation Proclamation and the change in Northern policy did not mean black soldiers were treated equally. Because Northerners were still queasy about "colored" soldiers, officers of colored regiments had to be white, and enlisted men could only attain non-commissioned officer status. It was not until early 1865 that a black soldier became a commissioned officer, when Sgt. Stephen A. Swails of the 54th Massachusetts was promoted to second lieutenant.

In addition, although told they would receive the same pay as white soldiers, the men of the 54th received reduced pay, from which additional money was withheld to cover the cost of clothing, which was not done in white regiments. Both the men and their officers refused to accept their wages until both black and white earned equal pay for equal work. The fight for equal pay lasted over a year, until the war was nearly over.

Black troops also faced unequal treatment from the enemy. When the 54th Massachusetts embarked on their journey south on May 28, 1863, they did so knowing that the Confederate Congress had announced that every captured black soldier would be sold into slavery, and every white officer in command of black troops would be executed. It was not until after the 54th went into battle, facing such treatment, that the United States government threatened retaliation on Confederate prisoners if the Confederacy went through with their word. ★

Battery Wagner

Situated on Morris Island, Battery Wagner's 30-foot-tall sloping walls were made of sand, turf, and palmetto logs. In front lay a moat 50 feet wide and filled with several feet of water. Felled trees with sharpened branches, called *abatis*, and boarding pikes ran along the moat. When the bombardment began, the Confederates piled sandbags around their artillery and then most of the soldiers hid in a giant bombproof shelter made of 12 inches of timber with 10 feet of sand on top. ★

At 8:15 A.M. on July 18, 1863, Union land and naval guns opened upon Battery Wagner, one of the defenses in Charleston Harbor, in one of the greatest bombardments of the Civil War. They kept firing until evening, when the Union infantry began its assault. At the lead stood the 54th Massachusetts.

Their brigade commander, Brig. Gen. George Strong, knew the men were worn out, but he had left the choice up to Shaw—if he wanted his men to take the place of honor in leading the assault upon the fort, they could. Colonel Shaw accepted the honor for his men. Though he ached for a chance for his men to prove they could fight, Shaw did not make the decision lightly. One of his captains recalled of him, "His bearing was composed and graceful; his cheek had somewhat paled; and the slight twitching of the corners of his mouth plainly showed that the whole cost was counted." The cost included himself. The night before, Shaw confided to Lt. Col. Edward Hallowell, "I do not believe I will live though our next fight."

Just before the regiment advanced, General Strong pointed to the man holding the national colors and asked, "If this man should fall, who will lift the flag and carry it on?"

Colonel Shaw calmly replied, "I will."

After the general rode away with his staff, Shaw told his men, "I want you to prove yourselves men. The eyes of thousands will look on what you do tonight."

Shaw divided the regiment into two lines of five companies each. He stood by the Stars and Stripes in the front line, while Hallowell stood next to the Massachusetts flag in the rear line. At 7:45 P.M., Colonel

"The eyes of thousands will look on what you do tonight."

Shaw raised his sword, and the 54th Massachusetts advanced. Threading in a V-shape down a narrow strip of beach between the Atlantic Ocean on the right and a swamp on the left, the regiment gradually increased speed and charged across a water-filled ditch, buried land mines, and sharpened stakes and up the slope of the fort in the face of artillery and rifle fire.

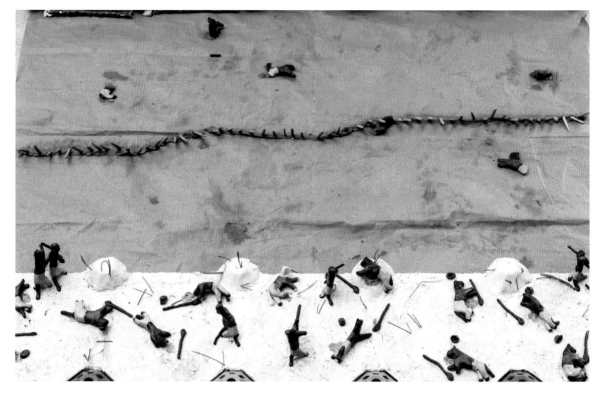

As their comrades fell, the men of the 54th Massachusetts closed ranks and pressed on. Hallowell later wrote of Colonel Shaw: "I saw him again, just for an instant, as he sprang into the ditch; his broken and shattered regiment were following him."

Shaw clambered up the slope of the fort with a knot of survivors, waved his sword and cried, "Forward, Fifty-fourth!" and fell into the fort with a bullet through his heart.

Col. Robert Gould Shaw

The men fought hand-to-hand, desperately hanging on against the 51st North Carolina and the Charleston Battalion, but support was slow in coming. The regiment had charged so quickly that no one realized they had entered the fort already. Some officers, including Lt. Edward B. Emerson, picked up rifles and began firing alongside their men. Beside Emerson, a soldier with a broken arm piled cartridges on his chest for the lieutenant to use.

Lt. Edward Emerson

By the time the regiment retreated, they had lost 281 men out of about 600. Of all the Union regiments involved on July 18, the 54th Massachusetts sustained the heaviest loss.

The regiments that advanced in waves behind the 54th Massachusetts could not take the fort. So the Union forces settled down for a siege. Late in 1863, the Confederates evacuated Battery Wagner.

The Confederates buried Colonel Shaw in a common grave with his men, possibly to insult him. However, Shaw's father refused to have the body recovered, choosing instead to leave his son where he had fallen with his men.

Sgt. William Carney

Taking up the 54th Massachusetts's national colors from the fallen color bearer, Sgt. William H. Carney planted the flag on the wall. Showing that he meant to stay, he knelt, gripping the flagstaff. Bullets tore into him, but he did not budge.

His comrades around him needed the courage they would gain from seeing their immovable colors. The colors were the heart of a regiment, and the 54th had the heart of a lion.

Carney did not move until the regiment fell back, and then, half crawling and covered with blood, he bore the colors safely from the field. By the time he reached the field hospital, he had been wounded in the breast, head, arm, and legs. He told his comrades, "I have only done my duty, the old flag never touched the ground."

Sergeant Carney received the Medal of Honor in 1900. Although other black soldiers were granted the award before him, Carney's was the earliest action for which the Medal of Honor was awarded to a black soldier. ★

Sgt. William H. Carney

Courage of Every Kind

The story of the 54th Massachusetts is one of courage—of every kind.

It takes courage to do the right thing, even if people think less of you because of it. When Shaw was offered command of a "colored" regiment, he chose what was best for the men of the 54th, instead of his own ego, to give them the chance to prove that they were no different than whites, to prove that they were, in fact, *men*.

It takes courage to keep going, despite an uncertain future. When the 54th headed south, they did not know if their government would defend them if they were captured. But they marched south anyway, determined to fight for their nation—even if it would not fight for them.

It takes courage to risk your life to save *another* person's life. In their first taste of combat, the 54th put their own lives on the line to save the trapped 10th Connecticut.

And then there is the courage exhibited on July 18, 1863.

After advancing through obstacles, artillery fire, and musketry, after climbing the sloping wall of Battery Wagner and seeing Colonel Shaw fall dead, the men of the 54th hung on, fighting unsupported. Despite losing nearly half of the regiment, they did not falter or give up on their mission.

Through their actions, the soldiers of the 54th Massachusetts not only proved themselves men, but they proved themselves to be men of the highest caliber. ★

Andersonville

O N FEBRUARY 27, 1864, A NEW PRISON CAMP IN GEORGIA OPENED its gates to Union prisoners of war. Although named Camp Sumter, the prison came to be known as Andersonville, after the nearby town of that name. Little did anyone know what a hell on earth it would become. Approximately 45,000 men passed through Andersonville. Of those men, 12,912 never saw freedom.

In early 1864, the new prison camp seemed a good answer to the problem of overcrowded prisons across the South. It was far away from threats of Union raids, and a small stream promised a constant supply of water for the prisoners.

A 15-foot-tall stockade with two gates enclosed 16½ acres that sloped down to the stream in the middle of the camp. Sentry boxes (called "pigeon roosts" by the prisoners) stood every 30 yards along the stockade. In early April, a fence of 4-foot-tall posts with a thin rail on top was built inside the camp, 19 feet from the stockade. Any prisoner crossing the "deadline" would be shot. Other prisons in both North and South had similar deadlines.

Andersonville was designed for 10,000 prisoners, but because the North had stopped exchanging prisoners of war in 1863, the prison was soon packed to overflowing. In June, the stockade was enlarged to 26 acres, but the expansion did little to relieve the overcrowding. By the end

> **No one knew what a hell on earth the new prison camp would become.**

of June, the prison held 23,307 men, and the numbers continued to rise to a peak of 33,000.

"This Hell on Earth"

Scale: 1:72   **Number of Cats:** US: 442; CS: 8

Dimensions: 4'7" x 2'4.5"

Date Created: April 2009–Sept. 25, 2009

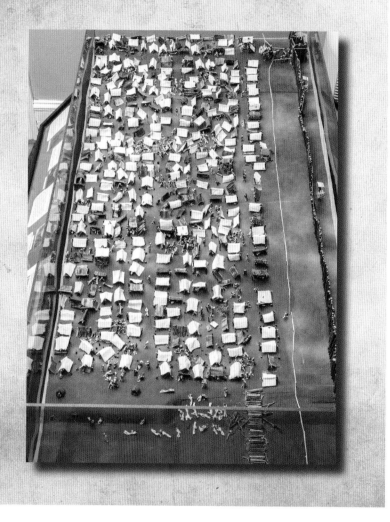

FROM THE START, CONDITIONS WERE FAR FROM SATISFACTORY.

Barracks for the prisoners were begun but never finished, partly for want of materials and partly because the commander of the camp, Capt. Henry Wirz, expected the prisoners to be exchanged before barracks were needed.

As a result, prisoners had to provide what shelter they could, resulting in thousands of "shebangs," ranging from tents to holes dug in the dirt. Prisoners used blankets,

Prisoners used blankets, overcoats, sticks, brush, and even coat linings for shelter.

overcoats, sticks, brush, and anything else they had, even the linings of their jackets.

Capt. Henry Wirz

Despite their situation, prisoners sought to create a semblance of ordinary life. Dirt mounds and stumps served as tables and chairs, and logs as pillows. Prisoners who had razors set up barbershops, complete with carved barber poles.

The Plight of POWs

Andersonville's story cannot be told without touching on the controversy that surrounds it. History will never settle the question of who is to blame for the suffering. After the war, blame fell on Captain Wirz, and he was arrested, tried, and hanged. However, in Wirz's defense, the Confederacy had trouble supplying food to its own army, much less to prisoners of war. Also, the overcrowding resulted from the break-down of exchange, which came about through Northern politicians and General Grant.

Ironically, conditions in Northern camps were no better, with Confederate prisoners freezing or starving to death in the land of plenty—because Congress passed a resolution setting forth a policy of retaliation on Confederate prisoners for conditions of Southern camps. In the land that history remembers as the good guys, POWs suffered and died because of spite.

Andersonville is an example of the huge, sticky mess of the treatment of POWs, where no one is completely innocent or completely guilty. Edward Boate, a prisoner at Andersonville, wrote after the war:

You rulers who make the charge that the rebels intentionally killed off our men, when I can honestly swear they were doing every thing in their power to sustain us, do not lay this flattering unction to your souls. You abandoned your brave men in the hour of their cruelest need. They fought for the Union, and you reached no hand out to save the old faithful, loyal, and devoted servants of the country. ★

The road from the North Gate, called Broadway or Main Street, was also known as Market Street because of the many prisoners hawking their goods—such as corn beer made from fermented cornmeal and water—and trading rations.

A barbershop

Rations at Andersonville consisted of ¼ pound of cornmeal (with the cob ground into it) and ⅓ pound of bacon or 1 pound of beef (often rotten). The rations came through the South Gate in a mule-drawn wagon every day—except when they did not come at all. Bags of cornmeal were thrown on the ground, and prisoners in charge of individual messes measured out cornmeal using tin cups. Each prisoner received one cupful. He then had several choices: he could eat it raw, cook it by himself, or combine it with rations from other prisoners and cook all the rations at once. This last method was the most common, because of the scarcity of firewood. The Confederates issued iron skillets to the prisoners, but only one skillet for every fifty men, so many prisoners used half-canteens or whatever other panlike objects they could find.

Even drinking water was hard to come by. The creek

A well

Daily rations were one cup of cornmeal and spoiled bacon.

entered the stockade already contaminated, having passed through the cookhouse and the Confederate guards' camp. Rain washed all the filth of the prison camp into the creek, and maggots filled the surrounding swamp until it heaved and rolled like ocean waves.

Some men dug wells as alternatives, but for most prisoners, the stream remained the only source of drinking and washing water. In August, after a terrible storm, a spring welled up inside the camp, providing clean water. The prisoners named it Providence Spring.

Prisoners spent their time sleeping, talking about exchange, and playing games such as poker, chess, and checkers. Others carved objects, particularly pipes, with intricate eagles, cannons, and other designs on the bowls. Some prisoners worked to tunnel under the stockade. While escape was generally unsuccessful, due to the guards' bloodhounds, prisoners never gave up trying. To hide the activity, prisoners often started tunnels inside shebangs.

Prisoners never gave up trying to escape by digging secret tunnels.

Pvt. Robert Sneden described how one man cut the clay with a knife, then scooped it between his legs. A man behind him packed it in a haversack and sent it out to others who carried it to the swamp to dump it inconspicuously. Due to the lack of ventilation, the tunneller sometimes ran out of fresh air and had to be pulled out, unconscious. As many as sixteen men might work on a tunnel, taking utmost care to avoid discovery, since fellow prisoners might tell the guards in order to secure favor.

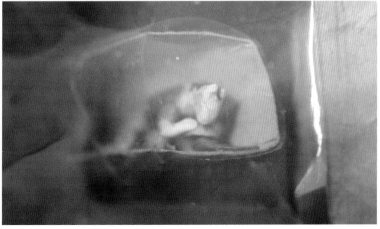

Top: Sneaking dirt away from the tunnel entrance

Right: Digging

The month of August 1864 averaged over a hundred dead per day.

The most common causes of death were diarrhea and dysentery, as the rations—particularly the corncobs in the meal—wrought havoc on prisoners' digestive tracts. Another major cause of death was scurvy, brought on by a lack of vitamin C. By the end of June, twenty-six men died every day. The month of August averaged over a hundred dead per day. Naked corpses lay rotting in a pile by the South Gate, waiting to be carried out.

Private Sneden recalled how one grew used to the death around him, to the point that prisoners would wait by a dying soldier so they could take what little clothes he had as soon as he died. Some even went so far as to kick a dying man while cursing, "d—n you why don't you die!" Many soldiers lost all hope of exchange or rescue, and lay down by the creek to die. Others intentionally approached the deadline in order to be shot.

A Touch of Christian Compassion

Unlike many outsiders who were afraid of the death and turned away by the stench, two Roman Catholic priests, Fathers William Hamilton and Peter Whelan, came into the stockade every Sunday to offer what comfort they could to the dying prisoners. Father Hamilton was diligent in giving extreme unction to the dying. Father Whelan spent four months of the summer, including August with the highest death rate, with the prisoners. When he left, he borrowed money to buy 10,000 pounds of wheat flour.

Father William Hamilton

This was baked and distributed at the hospital for several months. The life-saving bread became known as "Whelan's bread." ★

Scurvy

The Raiders were another threat to prisoners' lives. Roaming in gangs of five to twenty and carrying weapons such as clubs hardened in fire, these prisoners robbed and murdered their fellow soldiers. They lived in groups throughout the camp and on an island in the swamp, where they could escape the other prisoners. By June, hardly an hour went by—even in the daytime—without a cry of "Raiders!" and an ensuing scuffle.

In late June, the prisoners organized a police force called the Regulators, led by a man called "Limber Jim." Over the first few days of July, the Regulators waged war against the Raiders. Over a hundred Raiders were arrested and, with Wirz's permission, tried before a judge and jury of fellow prisoners. Many were sentenced to "run the gauntlet" or suffer similar punishments. On July 11, six of the leaders were hanged.

In September, any prisoners well enough to be moved were transferred to other prisons, to keep them away from Gen. William Tecumseh Sherman's Union army, which had just taken Atlanta. But Andersonville had already become the hellhole that history would forever remember and condemn.

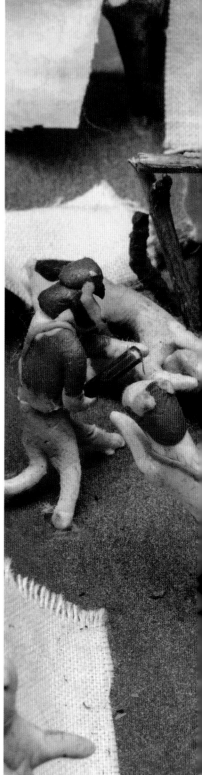

"Raiders!"

Pvt. Luke W. Brown, 8th Pennsylvania Cavalry

In 2009, we began our diorama of Andersonville in honor of Luke W. Brown, the half-brother of our great-great-grandfather Elmer. He lived in Millville, New Jersey with his mother and siblings, and after his father's death in 1859, he was the man of the house. He stood 5-feet 7-inches tall, with brown hair, blue eyes, and a fair complexion. He worked as a glassblower.

In September 1861, at the age of seventeen, Luke traveled to Philadelphia and enlisted in the 8th Pennsylvania Cavalry. He was captured in June 1863 and paroled in July. That October, the 8th Pennsylvania was involved in a fight near Warrenton, Virginia. The regiment ran low on ammunition, but their request for more was denied. As Confederate cavalry bore down on them, the Union troopers tossed aside their empty carbines and used their revolvers. The 8th was overwhelmed,

Pvt. Luke W. Brown AUTHORS' COLLECTION

and many, including Luke, were captured.

Records say that Luke died at Andersonville on either July 9 or

September 9, 1864. The different causes of death—starvation, scurvy, diarrhea, and gunshot wound—probably reflect various

Elmer Brown

AUTHORS' COLLECTION

**Luke Brown (seated) and
William Gilchrist, of the 2nd
West Virginia Veteran Infantry**

aspects of the same root cause: scurvy. Not only can it bring on diarrhea, but scurvy can reopen old wounds since the body is unable to properly maintain scar tissue.

Only nine years old when his brother died, Elmer never forgot the last time he watched Luke ride away. When he grew up, he named his son after the brother who never came home. Our family has had a Luke Brown ever since, through five generations. ★

Moving Toward Healing

ON APRIL 9, 1865, GENERAL LEE'S ARMY OF NORTHERN VIRGINIA surrendered to General Grant at Appomattox Court House, Virginia. Although other Confederate armies continued to fight, the Civil War was for all intents and purposes over. As the victor, Grant could offer any terms of surrender he liked. He was already famous as "Unconditional Surrender" Grant, after the surrender of Fort Donelson in 1862. He could have demanded the same unconditional surrender from Lee.

But Grant recognized that the Confederate soldiers were now his countrymen again. He gave them generous terms, and every decision he made was designed to promote recovery and peace. He allowed the Confederates to take their horses and mules home to work their farms. As news of the surrender spread through the army, he ordered his men not to cheer, so the Confederates were not further humiliated. He even had rations issued to the starving Southerners. Because Grant saw his enemy as human beings and not just defeated foes, healing began immediately.

> ## As victor, Grant could offer any terms of surrender he liked.

Honor Answering Honor

On April 12, the Confederates marched past the Union Army of the Potomac to lay down their arms. As the head of the column under Maj. Gen. John Gordon began to pass by, Maj. Gen. Joshua Chamberlain gave an order, a bugle sounded, and the Union soldiers stood at attention, shifting their rifles to "carry arms"—a military salute. Catching the meaning, Gordon wheeled his horse and saluted, then ordered his men to "carry arms" in reply. It was, Chamberlain wrote, "honor answering honor." ★

The Dioramas

EACH OF OUR DIORAMAS IS INSPIRED BY A STORY THAT EVOKES EMOTION. Sometimes, the story involves smaller individual tales happening over a period of time. Since each diorama portrays only one point in time, we have to select the tale with the most dramatic, emotional, or educational value.

We want our dioramas to be as historically accurate as possible, within the limitations of our materials and scale. So, when researching, we pay particular attention to minor details. For example, General Garnett waved his black hat while advancing during Pickett's Charge. Missing that detail would mean making him with the default—a sword—in his hand.

To show what the action might have looked like, we

¾-inch cannon for Hazlett with two cats, 1-inch cat, 2-inch cat

take into account regimental strengths and casualties. Casualty totals from after a battle are useful, and sometimes soldiers' accounts give an idea of their losses. If we cannot find actual numbers, we use general rules of thumb, such as four men wounded for every man killed.

REBECCA BECAME INTERESTED IN PICKETT'S CHARGE after reading McKinley Kantor's *Gettysburg*. As a result, one of our earliest dioramas portrayed the entire Confederate line as they fought at the stone wall. As time passed, we wanted to make

We select the most dramatic, emotional, or educational stories to tell.

it closer to scale. We shrank the cats and doubled the diorama's width, but even then it was not large enough, so we added boxes to extend it all around. In 2000, our father suggested we make a to-scale, topographical version of

Pickett's Charge. Since the whole line would not fit in the available space, we decided to focus on the fighting at the Angle.

Using a set of topographical maps, we made the ground from layers of foam insulation and covered the surface with a plasterlike compound to protect it. Since we did not know about foam ground cover yet, we painted the surface green and supplemented it with little bushes. Referring to the maps for the location and type of period fences and walls, we made post-and-rail fences from toothpicks and built the stone wall with countless clay rocks.

Finding Connections

When making dioramas, sometimes you find interesting connections between facts, which might otherwise go unnoticed. Rebecca's research for "The Fate of Gettysburg" led her to a conclusion that we have not seen in any of our reading.

It all began with accounts by Colonel Mayo of the 3rd Virginia and Corporal Carter of the 53rd Virginia. Before the advance began, Mayo saw his brigade commander General Kemper ride past on "his mettlesome sorrel." After Armistead's brigade crossed the Emmitsburg Road, Carter (whose regiment was in the center, behind General Armistead) saw Kemper ride up to Armistead on "a handsome bay." The conflicting descriptions puzzled Rebecca. Back then, people would know the difference between a sorrel and a bay: brown with no black, or brown with black points, respectively.

Why does it matter? Well, reconciling these accounts does more than tell us which color horse to put the general on. It may also give insight into Kemper's location when he was wounded.

Some accounts of Kemper's wounding placed him near the Codori farm, about two-thirds of the way across the fields. Others, including that of General Kemper himself, placed him close to the stone wall when he fell. Some say he and his horse went down, while others say he fell into the arms of his mounted orderly, suggesting two different episodes.

Rebecca's theory is that General Kemper started the charge on his sorrel, which fell at the Codori farm. Soldiers saw him (and his horse) go down and then did not notice him get up and mount a bay. Later, others saw him on the bay as they approached the wall. Finally, Kemper himself fell wounded near the stone wall. ★

Rebecca estimated how many cats to make, using Confederate brigade strengths and casualty totals. She also looked at other factors, such as what percentage of the whole field is covered by the diorama, and the fact that higher casualties would occur as the Confederates approached the wall. Even though the calculations were estimates, viewers of the diorama still get a sense of what the fighting might have looked like.

Making the cats, Rebecca cranked out over a thousand Confederates at five minutes each, while Ruth spent half an hour on each cat of the 72nd Pennsylvania—fifteen minutes for the basic cat with leggings and fifteen minutes for the red piping and buttons on their coats.

In 2011, we overhauled the diorama and glued turf on top of the green paint. We added Cushing's dead and wounded artillery horses, debris from exploded limbers and caissons, and more cats fighting in the Copse. Because of Stannard's flanking movement, most of Pickett's division would have been along the stone wall portrayed on our diorama, so we added more than a thousand Confederates.

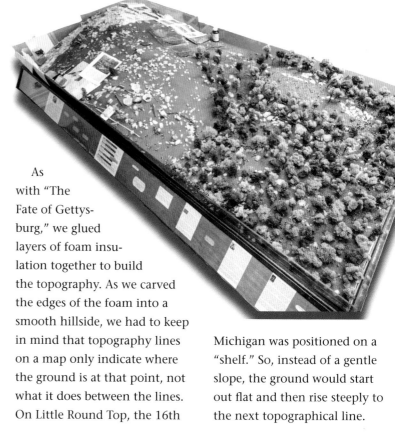

THE INITIAL INSPIRA-
TION FOR "THE BOYS
ARE STILL THERE" came
from the stories of Lieutenant
Hazlett's determination and
Colonel O'Rorke's gallantry.
But we had to decide exactly
what point in time—and therefore which stories—to portray.
While researching, we realized
that most of our favorite stories happened at the same time.
Just before the 20th Maine
charged, Colonel Chamber-
lain heard a "great roar" behind
them—probably O'Rorke's 140th
New York coming in. Hazlett's
guns cut through the New
Yorkers' column and some of
the infantrymen helped wrestle the guns up the slope.

As
with "The
Fate of Gettys-
burg," we glued
layers of foam insu-
lation together to build
the topography. As we carved
the edges of the foam into a
smooth hillside, we had to keep
in mind that topography lines
on a map only indicate where
the ground is at that point, not
what it does between the lines.
On Little Round Top, the 16th

Michigan was positioned on a
"shelf." So, instead of a gentle
slope, the ground would start
out flat and then rise steeply to
the next topographical line.

We covered the surface with plaster cloth to protect the foam and give us a good base to glue features onto. Rebecca used pencil, string, and strips of paper to mark the positions of rocks, the tree line, and troops. Period photos of specific areas along the crest show which rocks have not changed over the years (and some that have). Photos taken in 1897 allowed us to place particular trees around the 83rd Pennsylvania's position. Other photos and accounts helped define the clearing in which the 20th Maine stood. Some period photos show the entire hill, but were less useful, given the distance and the foreshortening that skews depth perception. As a result, Rebecca used photos of the present-day rock formations. Online aerial photos proved invaluable in spacing out the rocks.

Rebecca shaped rocks out of a white air-drying clay, which she then painted with a thin black acrylic wash. The paint darkened the crevices of the rocks, giving them a realistic look. Once the rocks were finished, Ruth sprayed the surface with a 50/50 glue and water mix, then sprinkled turf over the area. After the first layer of glue dried, a second coat anchored the turf.

Little Round Top had young trees in 1863, so Ruth selected twigs for tree trunks that were not so long or thick as to look like full-grown trees. For each tree, she glued clumps of reindeer moss to a twig, cradled it gently until the glue set, then hung the tree upside-down to finish drying without flattening the moss. To install the tree, she poked a hole in the plaster cloth and foam, dabbed glue into it, and gently pushed the trunk in, about half an inch deep. She also sprinkled dried black tea underneath the trees as fallen leaves.

Ruth applying turf

Rebecca placed the cats, beginning with the 20th Maine and progressing along Vincent's line, with the Confederates facing them. When finished, "The Boys Are Still There" will feature several thousand soldiers, including dozens of identified officers and men. While Hazlett's cannons and Vincent's battle line are a major part of the diorama, they are not all of it. Other details include stretcher bearers and wounded men heading for the rear, several aid stations, a Signal Corps station, Hazlett's limbers and caissons, and possibly an ambulance.

Rebecca gluing down cats

Less is More

Level of detail is a big consideration when making a diorama. Our cats do not carry canteens, cap boxes, or cartridge boxes because putting every detail on a model can make it look cluttered. Including canteens on "The Boys Are Still There" would have told the story of the 15th Alabama's missing canteens, but would have overloaded the cats visually.

However, sometimes we *can* add details that bring attention to a particular aspect. On our Little Round Top diorama, we included corps badges because one regiment wore a different color badge. This allows us to explain one way that Union soldiers were identified. ★

WHEN DESIGNING OUR DIORAMA OF THE IRONCLADS, we wanted to select a point in time when the two ships were close to each other, even touching. This would show how intense the battle became, while also making the diorama compact. We decided on the moment when *Monitor* fired both guns at point-blank range and the concussion sent *Virginia*'s gun crews reeling, stunned and bleeding.

Rebecca created both ships out of a combination of wood and cardboard. We used period sketches and descriptions of *Virginia*, along with artistic depictions. Photos of later ironclads of similar design helped to fill in gaps about features, like the covers for her gun ports, only two of which were installed at the time of her first battle. We recreated the different types of guns on *Virginia* and, where possible, identified the locations of each. We also noted the damage from the first day's fighting, such as the two guns with damaged barrels and the missing boats and ram.

For *Monitor*, we used photographs of the ship herself as well as detailed descriptions and plans. Importantly, *Monitor*'s turret and other artifacts have been raised from the ship's final resting place. So, using photographs for reference, we re-created the turret's interior structure and details such as the lanterns.

One question we faced when making a diorama of ships was whether to depict only the portions above the waterline or to find a way of suspending complete ships in "water." We

A lantern in *Monitor*'s turret AUTHORS' COLLECTION

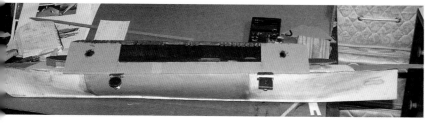

***Virginia* under construction**
AUTHORS' COLLECTION

The Accuracy is in the Details

Any diorama has details specific to the scene that a casual observer may not notice or appreciate, but that the makers need to get right in order to create an accurate and informative depiction. Here are a few examples.

In "The Bombardment of Fort Sumter," the flag flies at half-staff after becoming stuck the day before.

In "The Horrid Creation of a Nightmare," *Virginia*'s crew wears blue uniforms, not gray. Navies traditionally wore blue uniforms, and it took a while for Confederate sailors to accept the notion of breaking with tradition. Eventually they switched to gray, but not before the two ironclads met.

In "The Boys Are Still There," fallen leaves cover the ground under the trees, but there is not much underbrush since farmers grazed cattle in the area.

In the case of "The Fate of Gettysburg," the diorama's story proves how important it is to pay attention to the overall story, in addition to the exact time portrayed. For ten years, we did not take morning artillery actions into account and therefore did not show the fallen horses and debris of Cushing's battery.

In "This Hell on Earth," we wanted to show what might happen on an average day inside the stockade: some prisoners playing poker, chess, and checkers, some building a new shebang (with the inevitable onlookers offering suggestions), and a few unfortunate souls who have knocked food into the fire and are getting cussed out for it. ★

decided to make the whole ships, from keel to smokestack. This allowed us to recreate features like the propellers, rudders, and *Monitor*'s unique anchor well, which was designed so her men could raise and lower the anchor from within the ship.

To achieve the look of suspension in water, we made a wooden box and painted the inside of it a varied blue, to give the "water" depth. Then, we cut holes for the ships in a sheet of Plexiglas and fitted it to the top of the box. Whereas *Virginia* is made as a complete unit and rests on short supports underneath her hull, *Monitor*'s hull is a separate piece from her deck. To suspend the smaller ironclad, we glued the hull to the underside of the Plexiglas.

Rebecca researched ships' wakes at various speeds, down to the slow speeds of the 6 to 8 knots at which these ironclads likely traveled, and calculated the spacing of ripples and the proper amount of turbulence. Then she did her best to determine what water would actually do, given the unusual shape of each ironclad. *Virginia*, even though built on a normal hull, has a strange shape at the waterline, with only the hulking casemate and the "breakwater" on her bow rising above the waves. *Monitor* has a completely unique design. Rebecca also looked at photographs of modern battleships firing their big guns, for ideas on how the concussion would affect the water.

Rebecca used gloss superheavy gel to form ripples and

waves, built up the bow-waves and turbulence, and flattened out the area for the guns' concussion. Ordinarily used to thicken paint, the gel dries clear and can be curled over into whitecaps, or smoothed into undulating ripples. When everything had dried, she painted white "foam" on top of the bow-waves and turbulence.

Finally, both ships needed smoke from their guns and coal-burning engines. White pillow stuffing served both purposes, after Ruth spray painted some of it black for the coal smoke. Even something as simple as smoke can tell a story. Black smoke puffs out of holes blown in *Virginia*'s smokestack during the previous day's fighting. White smoke from *Virginia*'s guns drifts away, indicating the moments that have elapsed since she fired, but *Monitor*'s smoke is concentrated as she fires at the very moment of the diorama.

WE HOPE YOU HAVE ENJOYED YOUR TOUR THROUGH the dioramas of Civil War Tails. Many more stories are waiting to come out of storage in the museum, and others await discovery in books. This is just the beginning, and we are excited to share the journey with you.

Glossary

ARMY ORGANIZATION

Company: the basic unit; nominally 100 men; due to losses during the war, in reality a company's strength would be less, perhaps even as low as a couple dozen men

Regiment: 10 companies; nominally 1,000 men; by Gettysburg, a typical regiment contained only 200–400 men

Brigade: 5 regiments

Division: 3 brigades

Corps (pronounced "core"): 3 divisions

Army: several corps; at Gettysburg, the Army of Northern Virginia had 3 corps, and the Army of the Potomac had 7

ARMY RANKS

Private: the lowest rank; an enlisted man

Corporal: the lowest non-commissioned rank

Sergeant: non-commissioned rank; higher than corporal

Lieutenant: the lowest commissioned rank; 2nd lieutenants are lower than 1st lieutenants

Captain: commanded a company

Major: during battle, helped the colonel by watching over the left wing

Lieutenant Colonel: during battle, helped the colonel by watching over the right wing

Colonel: commanded a regiment

Brigadier General: commanded a brigade

Major General: in the Confederate armies, commanded a division; in the Union armies, commanded a division, corps, or army

Lieutenant General: in the Confederate armies, commanded a corps; the Union did not have this rank until Congress revived it for General Grant

ARTILLERY

Ammunition

Canister: a can that would explode upon firing, scattering 1.5-inch iron balls; effective against infantry at close range; double canister meant ramming two shots down the barrel; treble canister meant using three

Case shot (spherical case, shrapnel): a shot containing musket balls, timed to explode over or in front of infantry; effective against advancing infantry

Shell: a shot with a fuse that was lit when the gun fired; used against earthworks or troops

Solid shot: a solid cannonball; useful for pounding a position, disabling enemy cannons, or bowling through massed infantry

Caisson: carried two ammunition chests and hooked to a limber, giving a cannon and its limber three backup chests

Depress: to aim a cannon as low as possible

Field of fire: the area in front of cannons where their view was not blocked, such as by trees

Limber: carried one ammunition chest for a cannon; for transportation, the cannon attached to the back of the limber; to unlimber meant to unhook the cannon

Naming: cannons were often named for the designer (Parrott, Brooke, Dahlgren) or their weight of shot (42-pounder); terms such as "3-inch" or "10-inch" referred to the size of the bore in their barrels

Rifling: grooves inside the barrel of a gun, which cause the bullet or shell to spin, giving it a longer range than a smoothbore gun

Types

3-inch Ordnance: a rifled cannon; most common in the Union army

Columbiad: a large cannon used in siege or naval artillery

Dahlgren: a large cannon with a distinctive soda bottle shape; used by the navy

Howitzer: any short-barreled, small cannon

Mortar: a cannon designed to shoot in a high trajectory over walls

Napoleon: a smoothbore cannon; most common in the Confederate army

Parrott: a rifled cannon; recognized by the band of reinforcing iron around its breech (the back end of the barrel)

Pivot gun: a naval cannon on a track so it could turn and fire in different directions

NAVAL TERMS

Aft or **after:** to the rear; on the stern of a ship

Division: on a ship, the guns were divided into divisions, each under an officer (similar to sections in a battery in the field artillery)

Draft: the depth of water a ship requires in order to float

Fore or **forward:** to the front; on the bow of a ship

Gun captain: the man in charge of a particular gun

Port: left

Starboard: right

MISCELLANEOUS TERMS

Battery: a type of fortification; also the basic unit of field artillery, made up of six cannons (the Confederates usually used four) divided into three sections of two guns each

Casemate: an armored enclosure (on ships) or a chamber (in forts) from which guns could be fired

Double-quick: a pace similar to a jog or trot; the men in Pickett's Charge began at the route step (a quick walk), then sped up to the double-quick as they drew nearer to the enemy, and then made a final rush to the stone wall

Embrasure: an opening in a wall through which a gun could fire

Esplanade: a long, level area outside a fortress wall, providing a place to walk and a clear field of fire

Flank: the end or side of something; to go around the end or side of something

Lanyard: a 12-foot rope used to fire a cannon; it was attached to a friction primer and when pulled would create a spark which lit the gunpowder

Notes

Chapter 2

"tangible evidence"—Robert Hendrickson, *Sumter: The First Day of the Civil War* (New York: Dell Publishing, 1990), 71.

"as I never"—W. A. Swanberg, *First Blood: The Story of Fort Sumter* (New York: Charles Scribner's Sons, 1957), 298.

"tramped on"—Swanberg, *First Blood*, 290.

Chapter 3

"that little thing"—James Tertius DeKay, *Monitor: The Story of the Legendary Civil War Ironclad and the Man Whose Invention Changed the Course of History* (New York: Walker, 1997), 183.

"no match"—A. A. Hoehling, *Damn the Torpedoes! Naval Incidents of the Civil War* (New York: Gramercy Books, 1998), 20.

"huge, half submerged"—DeKay, *Monitor*, 164.

"the reverse"—Hoehling, *Damn the Torpedoes*, 20.

"small and trifling"—Hoehling, *Damn the Torpedoes*, 20.

"insignificant . . . a speck"—William C. Davis, *Duel Between the First Ironclads* (Mechanicsburg, PA: Stackpole Books, 1994), 112.

"we did not"—Davis, *Duel*, 118.

"like chickens"—R. Thomas Campbell, *Gray Thunder: Exploits of the Confederate States Navy* (Shippensburg, PA: Burd Street Press, 1996), 32.

"handsome gun deck"—Ivan Musicant, *Divided Waters: The Naval History of the Civil War* (Edison, NJ: Castle Books, 2000), 136.

"weird and mysterious"—DeKay, *Monitor*, 164.

"no more effect"—DeKay, *Monitor*, 164.

"It seemed she"—DeKay, *Monitor*, 166.

"Jack, don't"—DeKay, *Monitor*, 167.

"No ship was"—DeKay, *Monitor*, 166.

"out of pity"—Musicant, *Divided Waters*, 153.

"All at once"—Davis, *Duel*, 110.

"What can that"—DeKay, *Monitor*, 183.

"I will stand"—Musicant, *Divided Waters*, 170.

"the strangest"—DeKay, *Monitor*, 185.

"immediately ran down"—Jack Greene and Alessandro Massignani, *Ironclads at War: The Origin and Development of the Armored Warship, 1854–1891* (Conshohocken, PA: Combined Publishing, 1998), 74.

"The most profound"—Davis, *Duel*, 120.

"Commence firing"—Davis, *Duel*, 120.

"You can see"—Davis, *Duel*, 120–21.

"rattling broadside"—Musicant, *Divided Waters*, 171.

"A look of confidence"—*Battles and Leaders of the Civil War* (Secaucus, NJ: Castle, 1887), 1:723.

"dropped over"—Davis, *Duel*, 129.

"when a gun"—*Battles and Leaders*, 1:725.

"our technical"—*Battles and Leaders*, 1:724.

"unwieldy as"—DeKay, *Monitor*, 193.

"would have permitted"—Musicant, *Divided Waters*, 153.

"heaped quick-burning"—Campbell, *Gray Thunder*, 46.

"We piled on"—Campbell, *Gray Thunder*, 46–47.

"one Samsonian effort"—Davis, *Duel*, 127.

"dragged herself"—Campbell, *Gray Thunder*, 47.

"Go ahead"—DeKay, *Monitor*, 193.

"It was really laughable"—Davis, *Duel*, 130.

"I cannot see"—Davis, *Duel*, 132.

Chapter 4

"seems cursed"—Garry E. Adelman and Timothy H. Smith, *Devil's Den: A History and Guide* (Gettysburg, PA: Thomas Publications, 1997), 9.

"tore gap after gap"—Adelman and Smith, *Devil's Den*, 25.

"Give them shell"—Harry W. Pfanz, *Gettysburg—The Second Day* (Chapel Hill: University of North Carolina Press, 1987), 186.

"My God, men"—Pfanz, *Gettysburg—The Second Day*, 187.

"For God's sake"—Pfanz, *Gettysburg—The Second Day*, 191.

"Captain Bigelow"—Bradley M. Gottfried, *The Artillery of Gettysburg* (Nashville: Cumberland House, 2008), 140.

"superhuman"—Gottfried, *Artillery*, 140.

"the enemy crowded"—Pfanz, *Gettysburg—The Second Day*, 344.

"I place you"—Joshua Lawrence Chamberlain, *Bayonet! Forward: My Civil War Reminiscences* (Gettysburg, PA: Stan Clark Military Books, 1994), 23.

"no place" (entire exchange)—Gottfried, *Artillery*, 116.

"each man"—Gottfried, *Artillery*, 116.

"I have since"—Gottfried, *Artillery*, 116.

"The calm"—Thomas A. Desjardin, *Stand Firm Ye Boys From Maine: The 20th Maine and the Gettysburg Campaign* (Gettysburg, PA: Thomas Publications, 1995), 56.

"There he sat"—Pfanz, *Gettysburg—The Second Day*, 224.

"queer notion"—Chamberlain, *Bayonet*, 31.

"By sheer force"—Chamberlain, *Bayonet*, 27.

"in the center"—Chamberlain, *Bayonet*, 29.

"No military music"—Gottfried, *Artillery*, 117.

"Down this way"—Pfanz, *Gettysburg—The Second Day*, 228.

"Here they are"—Pfanz, *Gettysburg—The Second Day*, 230.

"No, brother"—Desjardin, *Stand Firm*, 40.

"Tell my folks"—Desjardin, *Stand Firm*, 112.

"dearest relative"—Desjardin, *Stand Firm*, 112.

"great roar"—Desjardin, *Stand Firm*, 68.

"Bayonet"—Chamberlain, *Bayonet*, 33.

"we ran"—Glenn Tucker, *High Tide at Gettysburg: The Campaign in Pennsylvania.* (Gettysburg, PA: Stan Clark Military Books, 1995), 265.

"The boys are"—Desjardin, *Stand Firm*, 106.

"Boys, I don't"—Chamberlain, *Bayonet*, 22.

"If ever I"—Desjardin, *Stand Firm*, 99.

"an opportunity"—Clark, *Gettysburg*, 75.

Chapter 5

"old war horse"—George R. Stewart, *Pickett's Charge: A Microhistory of the Final Attack at Gettysburg, July 3, 1863* (Boston: Houghton Mifflin, 1987), 17.

"no fifteen thousand"—Jeffry D. Wert, *Gettysburg: Day Three* (New York: Simon & Schuster, 2001), 102.

"Many of these"—Wert, *Gettysburg*, 128.

"inside of"—Wert, *Gettysburg*, 121.

"old and tough"—Clark, *Gettysburg*, 133.

"seem[ed] to say"—Wert, *Gettysburg*, 171.

"cool as a"—Wert, *Gettysburg*, 149.

"One felt safe"—Tucker, *High Tide*, 193.

"There are times" (full exchange)—Clark, *Gettysburg*, 133.

"found courage"—Stewart, *Pickett's Charge*, 130.

"The 18 guns"—Stewart, *Pickett's Charge*, 158.

"General, shall I" (full exchange)—Stewart, *Pickett's Charge*, 164.

"Every size"—Richard Rollins, ed., *Pickett's Charge! Eyewitness Accounts* (Redondo Beach, FL: Rank and File Publications, 1996), 379.

"centered in"—Timothy H. Smith, compiler, *Farms at Gettysburg: The Fields of Battle: Selected Images from the Adams County Historical Society* (Gettysburg, PA: Thomas Publications, 2007), 41.

"Up, men"—Kathy Georg Harrison and John W. Busey, *Nothing But Glory: Pickett's Division at Gettysburg* (Gettysburg, PA: Thomas Publications, 1993), 39.

"remember your wives"—Harrison and Busey, *Nothing But Glory*, 56.

"Sergeant, I want you" (full exchange)—Rollins, ed., *Pickett's Charge*, 193.

"The whole column"—Harrison and Busey, *Nothing But Glory*, 50.

"I can see no end"—Gottfried, *Artillery*, 216.

"The crash of shell"—Rollins, ed., *Pickett's Charge*, 179.

"lazy and lackadaisical" (full exchange)—Rollins, ed., *Pickett's Charge*, 158.

"Faster, men"—Tucker, *High Tide*, 362–64.

"Cease firing"—Tucker, *High Tide*, 362.

"Don't shoot him"—Stewart, *Pickett's Charge*, 197.

"General, hurry up"—Tucker, *High Tide*, 362.

"There are the guns"—Stewart, *Pickett's Charge*, 205.

"everything was"—Rollins, ed., *Pickett's Charge*, 159.

"The fate"—Col. Frank A. Haskell, *The Battle of Gettysburg* (Sandwich, MA: Chapman Billies, 1993), 91.

"like the hooded"—Rollins, ed., *Pickett's Charge*, 159.

"My brave horse" (entire discussion of Dick)—Haskell, *The Battle of Gettysburg*, 122–23.

"a hasty trench"—Rollins, ed., *Pickett's Charge*, 171.

"Go on"—Stewart, *Pickett's Charge*, 203.

"We have been"—Stewart, *Pickett's Charge*, 204.

"Give them"—Tucker, *High Tide*, 365.

"Who will follow"—Stewart, *Pickett's Charge*, 216-17.

"See, general" (full exchange)—Stewart, *Pickett's Charge*, 220.

"We followed"—Stewart, *Pickett's Charge*, 218.

"Everybody was loading"—Stewart, *Pickett's Charge*, 218.

"They are ours"—Harrison and Busey, *Nothing But Glory*, 91.

"Turn the guns"—Harrison and Busey, *Nothing But Glory*, 110.

"fairly jammed"—Rollins, ed., *Pickett's Charge*, 227.

"Whichever side"—Stewart, *Pickett's Charge*, 237.

"This was one"—Rollins, ed., *Pickett's Charge*, 227.

"could see nothing"—Harrison and Busey, *Nothing But Glory*, 72.

"Douthat" (full exchange)—Harrison and Busey, *Nothing But Glory*, 99.

"asked me"—Rollins, ed., *Pickett's Charge*, 159.

"It's all my fault"—Stewart, *Pickett's Charge*, 257.

"General Lee"—Stewart, *Pickett's Charge*, 256.

"We gained nothing"—Harrison and Busey, *Nothing But Glory*, 100.

"The first thing"—Bell Irvin Wiley, *The Life of Billy Yank: The Common Soldier of the Union* (Baton Rouge: Louisiana State University Press, 2000), 54.

"left no distinctive"—James I. Robertson, Jr., *The Civil War: Tenting Tonight* (Alexandria: Time-Life Books, 1984), 87.

"A spirit"—"Brady," accessed March 29, 2017, http://users.dickinson.edu/~osborne/404_98/whitep.htm.

"Let him who"—"Brady."

"If he has not"—"Brady."

Chapter 6

"white man's war"—Noah Andre Trudeau, *Like Men of War: Black Troops in the Civil War, 1862–1865* (Boston: Little, Brown, 1998), 8.

"a *white man's* government"—Clinton Cox, *Undying Glory: The Story of the Massachusetts 54th Regiment* (New York: Scholastic, 1991), 3.

"received into"—Cox, *Undying Glory*, 10.

"think I am"—Russell Duncan, ed., *Blue-Eyed Child of Fortune: The Civil War Letters of Col. Robert Gould Shaw* (New York: Avon Books, 1992), 283.

"Tell Mother"—Duncan, ed., *Blue-Eyed Child*, 287.

"But for the"—Cox, *Undying Glory*, 62.

"Well done"—Luis F. Emilio, *A Brave Black Regiment: The History of the 54th Massachusetts, 1863-1865* (New York: Da Capo Press, 1995), 67

"Hurrah, boys"—Emilio, *A Brave Black Regiment*, 67

"His bearing"—Emilio, *A Brave Black Regiment*, 78.

"I do not believe"—Cox, *Undying Glory*, 72.

"If this man" (full exchange)—Cox, *Undying Glory*, 77.

"I want you"—Emilio, *A Brave Black Regiment*, 78

"The eyes of thousands"—Cox, *Undying Glory*, 78.

"I saw him"—Peter Burchard, *One Gallant Rush: Robert Gould Shaw and His Brave Black Regiment* (New York: St. Martin's Press, 1965), 138.

"Forward"—Emilio, *A Brave Black Regiment*, 82.

"I have only"—Trudeau, *Like Men of War*, 84–85.

Chapter 7

"You rulers"—J. H. Segars, ed., *Andersonville: The Southern Perspective* (Atlanta: Southern Heritage Press, 1995), 190.

"d—n you"—Robert Knox Sneden, *Eye of the Storm*, edited by Charles F. Bryan, Jr. and Nelson D. Lankford (New York: Free Press, 2000), 229.

Chapter 8

"honor answering"—Chamberlain, *Bayonet*, 155.

The Dioramas

"his mettlesome"—Rollins, ed., *Pickett's Charge*, 158.

"a handsome"—Rollins, ed., *Pickett's Charge*, 193.

Bibliography & Suggested Reading

FORT SUMTER

Hendrickson, Robert. *Sumter: The First Day of the Civil War*. New York: Dell Publishing, 1990.

Swanberg, W. A. *First Blood: The Story of Fort Sumter*. New York: Charles Scribner's Sons, 1957.

THE IRONCLADS

Battles and Leaders of the Civil War. Vol. 1. Secaucus, NJ: Castle, 1887.

Campbell, R. Thomas. *Gray Thunder: Exploits of the Confederate States Navy*. Shippensburg, PA: Burd Street Press, 1996.

Davis, William C. *Duel Between the First Ironclads*. Mechanicsburg, PA: Stackpole Books, 1994.

DeKay, James Tertius. *Monitor: The Story of the Legendary Civil War Ironclad and the Man Whose Invention Changed the Course of History*. New York: Walker, 1997.

Greene, Jack, and Alessandro Massignani. *Ironclads at War: The Origin and Development of the Armored Warship, 1854–1891*. Conshohocken, PA: Combined Publishing, 1998.

Hoehling, A. A. *Damn the Torpedoes! Naval Incidents of the Civil War*. New York: Gramercy Books, 1998.

Musicant, Ivan. *Divided Waters: The Naval History of the Civil War*. Edison, NJ: Castle Books, 2000.

Still, William N. Jr., John M. Taylor, and Norman C. Delaney. *Raiders and Blockaders: The American Civil War Afloat*. Washington, DC: Brassey's, 1998.

GETTYSBURG

Adelman, Garry E., and Timothy H. Smith. *Devil's Den: A History and Guide*. Gettysburg, PA: Thomas Publications, 1997.

Brown, Kent Masterson. *Cushing of Gettysburg: The Story of a Union Artillery Commander*. Lexington: University Press of Kentucky, 1993.

Chamberlain, Joshua Lawrence. *Bayonet! Forward: My Civil War Reminiscences*. Gettysburg, PA: Stan Clark Military Books, 1994.

Clark, Champ. *The Civil War: Gettysburg—The Confederate High Tide*. Alexandria: Time-Life Books, 1985.

Coddington, Edwin B. *The Gettysburg Campaign: A Study in Command*. New York: Simon & Schuster, 1997.

Collins, Mary Ruth, and Cindy A. Stouffer. *One Soldier's Legacy: The National Homestead at Gettysburg*. Gettysburg, PA: Thomas Publications, 1993.

Desjardin, Thomas A. *Stand Firm Ye Boys From Maine: The 20th Maine and the Gettysburg Campaign*. Gettysburg, PA: Thomas Publications, 1995.

Ernsberger, Don. *At the Wall: The 69th Pennsylvania "Irish Volunteers" at Gettysburg*. Bloomington: Xlibris, 2006.

Georg Harrison, Kathy, and John W. Busey. *Nothing But Glory: Pickett's Division at Gettysburg*. Gettysburg, PA: Thomas Publications, 1993.

Gottfried, Bradley M. *The Artillery of Gettysburg*. Nashville: Cumberland House, 2008.

Haskell, Col. Frank A. *The Battle of Gettysburg*. Sandwich, MA: Chapman Billies, 1993.

Pfanz, Harry W. *Gettysburg—Culp's Hill and Cemetery Hill*. Chapel Hill: University of North Carolina Press, 1993.

Pfanz, Harry W. *Gettysburg—The First Day*. Chapel Hill: University of North Carolina Press, 2001.

Pfanz, Harry W. *Gettysburg—The Second Day*. Chapel Hill: University of North Carolina Press, 1987.

Rollins, Richard, ed. *Pickett's Charge! Eyewitness Accounts*. Redondo Beach, FL: Rank and File Publications, 1996.

Smith, Timothy H., compiler. *Farms at Gettysburg: The Fields of Battle: Selected Images from the Adams County Historical Society*. Gettysburg, PA: Thomas Publications, 2007.

Stewart, George R. *Pickett's Charge: A Microhistory of the Final Attack at Gettysburg, July 3, 1863*. Boston: Houghton Mifflin, 1987.

Tucker, Glenn. *High Tide at Gettysburg: The Campaign in Pennsylvania*. Gettysburg, PA: Stan Clark Military Books, 1995.

Wert, Jeffry D. *Gettysburg: Day Three*. New York: Simon & Schuster, 2001.

BATTERY WAGNER

Burchard, Peter. *One Gallant Rush: Robert Gould Shaw and His Brave Black Regiment*. New York: St. Martin's Press, 1965.

Cox, Clinton. *Undying Glory: The Story of the Massachusetts 54th Regiment*. New York: Scholastic, 1991.

Duncan, Russell, ed. *Blue-Eyed Child of Fortune: The Civil War Letters of Col. Robert Gould Shaw*. New York: Avon Books, 1992.

Emilio, Luis F. *A Brave Black Regiment: The History of the 54th Massachusetts, 1863–1865*. New York: Da Capo Press, 1995.

Katcher, Philip. *Lethal Glory: Dramatic Defeats of the Civil War*. London: Arms and Armour, 1997.

Trudeau, Noah Andre. *Like Men of War: Black Troops in the Civil War, 1862–1865*. Boston: Little, Brown, 1998.

ANDERSONVILLE / PVT. LUKE BROWN

Baldwin, Terry E. "Clerk of the Dead: Dorence Atwater." *Civil War Times Illustrated*, October 1971, 12–21.

Broomfield, William. "My Imprisonment Down in Dixie." Edited by Richard E. Shue. *Civil War Times Illustrated*, January 1989, 26-33.

Civil War Veterans' Card File, 1861–1866. Series #19.12. Record Group 19. Pennsylvania State Archives.

Coddington, Ronald S. "Out of Ammunition at Sulphur Springs." *Disunion*. October 13, 2013. Accessed March 27, 2017. https://opinionator. blogs.nytimes.com/2013/10/13/ out-of-ammunition-at-sulphur-springs/?_r=1.

Davis, Robert S. "Escape from Andersonville: A Study in Isolation and Imprisonment." *The Journal of Military History* 67.4 (2003): 1065.

"Food in Antarctica–page 2." *Cool Antarctica*. Last modified October 22, 2005. Accessed October 25, 2005. http://www.coolantarctica.com/Antarctica%20fact%20file/science/food2.htm.

Harris, Joseph K. "A Soldier's Narrative." *Civil War Times Illustrated*. May 1988, 36–41.

Mallison, David L. "The Andersonville Raiders." *Civil War Times Illustrated*. July 1971, 24–31.

Morsberger, Robert E. and Katherine M. Morsberger. "After Andersonville: The First War Crimes Trial." *Civil War Times Illustrated*. July 1974, 30–41.

National Park Service. "Andersonville: Prisoner of War Camp." *Teaching With Historic Places Lesson Plans*. Accessed February 28, 2005. http://www.cr.nps.gov/nr/twhp/wwwlps/lessons/11andersonville/11andersonville.htm.

Risdon, David. Brown family photos, family tree, and additional family research.

Segars, J. H., ed. *Andersonville: The Southern Perspective*. Atlanta: Southern Heritage Press, 1995.

Shewmon, Joe. "The Amazing Ordeal of Pvt. Joe Shewmon: Part I." *Civil War Times Illustrated*. April 1962, 45–50.

Sneden, Robert Knox. *Eye of the Storm*. Edited by Charles F. Bryan, Jr. and Nelson D. Lankford. New York: Free Press, 2000.

Sneden, Robert Knox. *Images from the Storm*. Edited by Charles F. Bryan, Jr., James C. Kelly, and Nelson D. Lankford. New York: Free Press, 2001.

MISCELLANEOUS

Catton, Bruce. *Grant Takes Command*. Boston: Little, Brown, 1969.

Coggins, Jack. *Arms and Equipment of the Civil War*. Mineola, MN: Dover Publications, 1990.

Dickinson College. "Brady." Accessed March 29, 2017. http://users.dickinson.edu/~osborne/404_98/whitep.htm.

Kukulski, Mike. "A Brief History of Photography: Part 4–Wet Plate Collodion." *Not Quite in Focus*. 21 January 2014. Accessed March 29, 2017. https://notquiteinfocus.com/2014/01/21/a-brief-history-of-photography-part-4-wet-plate-collodian/.

Miller, Francis Trevelyan, ed. *The Photographic History of The Civil War: in ten volumes, Thousands of Scenes Photographed 1861–65, with Text by many Special Authorities, Volume 1: The Opening Battles*. New York: Review of Reviews, 1912. Accessed March 29, 2017. http://www.perseus.tufts.edu/hopper/text?doc=Perseus%3Atext%3A2001.05.0106%3Achapter%3D2.4.

Robertson, James I., Jr. *The Civil War: Tenting Tonight*. Alexandria: Time-Life Books, 1984.

Wiley, Bell Irvin. *The Life of Billy Yank: The Common Soldier of the Union*. Baton Rouge: Louisiana State University Press, 2000.

Woodhead, Henry, ed. *Voices of the Civil War: Soldier Life*. Alexandria: Time-Life Books, 1996.

About the Authors

Twin sisters Ruth and Rebecca Brown have merged their interest in Civil War military history with their love for molding miniature soldiers in clay. On display at their unusual museum in Gettysburg, PA are dozens of historical dioramas and the 8,000 Union and Confederate CAT SOLDIERS they've created over the past twenty years. Their work and the museum, Civil War Tails at the Homestead Diorama Museum, have been featured in many articles, interviews,

and online videos, including the *Washington Post*, National Public Radio and CNN.

Ruth (*right*) works as an attorney and writes fantasy novels when she's not making trees or Yankees for the dioramas. Rebecca (*left*) gives tours of the museum and in her spare time, when not making more model cats, enjoys working on WWII and tall ship model kits, writing historical fiction, and watching old westerns. They live in Gettysburg, PA.